A Leap
of Faith

True stories for young and old

Peter J. Dyck

HERALD PRESS
Scottdale, Pennsylvania
Waterloo, Ontario

Library of Congress Cataloging-in-Publication Data
Dyck, Peter J., 1914-
   A leap of faith : true stories for young and old / Peter J.
Dyck.
     p.   cm.
   ISBN 0-8361-3523-7
   1. Dyck, Peter J., 1914-   .   2. Peace—Religious aspects—
Christianity.   I. Title.
BX8143.D93A3   1990
248.4—dc20   90-32837
                                         CIP

A LEAP OF FAITH
Copyright © 1990 by Herald Press, Scottdale, Pa. 15683
   Published simultaneously in Canada by Herald Press,
   Waterloo, Ont. N2L 6H7. All rights reserved.
Library of Congress Catalog Number: 90-32837
International Standard Book Number: 0-8361-3523-7
Printed in the United States of America
Design by Merrill R. Miller

1 2 3 4 5 6 7 8 9 10 96 95 94 93 92 91 90

To our grandchildren:
Peter, Deborah, Cory, Sasha, and Misha

Contents

Author's Preface

I write stories for our grandchildren. Come Christmas I gather what I've written during the year and presto, there's my Christmas gift for them. Then the "accident" happened.

To make sure I had gotten the facts straight, I sent the first draft of the Russian commentary story, which I titled "A Leap of Faith", to Walter Sawatsky. He and I had been intimately involved in the commentary project. Walter responded, but without asking me, sent a copy of his letter to Scottdale saying, "I hope Herald Press publishes it." They, in turn, said, "Where's the story?" So I sent it to them. Then they said, "That's not enough for a book. Send us some more stories."

Whether by "accident" or Providence, the stories originally written only for our five grandchildren will now be in the hands of many children. Ours gave their permission to share them with other boys and girls. However, it seems to me that they and their parents have a right to know why I write stories. Here are some of the reasons.

To make our grandchildren happy. Stories are fun. We read some of them aloud and others they read by themselves. By now I know which are their favorites because they ask to hear them again and again.

I also write to inform, to educate. Children want to learn. They're eager to find out things they don't know. For example, very few children under ten have ever thought about smuggling. What exactly does that mean? Is it right or wrong to smuggle? Is it right sometimes but wrong at other times? Is smuggling the same as cheating and lying?

And then I write to motivate, to mold character. I want my stories to be interesting, to be fun, but I don't write only to entertain. I'm concerned about passing on the faith. In one of my Christmas books I made for my grandchildren, I wrote in the foreword that I like to think of myself as a sower: "I sow words and ideas like a sower sows grain . . . And I also pray for a harvest, like peace and love, justice and compassion. . . ." I wanted our grandchildren to know that, so I was open about it.

The stories in this volume are basically true. Most of them are based on personal experiences. But I've written other stories, like *The Great Shalom* (also published by Herald Press), for example, which are pure fiction. However, even in the stories of this book some details are fictitious. For example, in "Ouch! That Hurts!" it's true that KM 81 in Paraguay is a Mennonite hospital for people with Hansen's disease (leprosy). I've been there many times. I checked out the facts with Dr. John Schmidt, the doctor who for many years worked there. I was careful to have the other nonmedical facts straight too. But the conversations between Pedro and the doctor or Pedro and Maria are imagined.

On the other hand, the story about Crete, titled "Here Stood Kandanos" (pronounced KONdonos), is true not only in basic fact but also in my conversations with Bishop Irineos and Klaus Froese.

Someone asked me how I feel about my stories? The answer is I feel good about them. But I always hope that the next one will be better.

—Peter J. Dyck
Akron, Pennsylvania

CHAPTER 1

A Leap of Faith

*T*he minister repeated what he had just finished saying. Sasha, listening carefully to the sermon, wondered why the minister kept repeating himself. Sitting with his parents on the hard bench of their plain church in Karaganda, the boy of ten pondered this. Did all the ministers in Russia do that in their preaching?

At home he asked his parents about it. They kept eating. They hesitated to answer.

Finally his mother wondered if the minister repeated himself because he thought what he had said was important. Being a kind woman, she didn't want to say anything that might hurt the pastor. "Your teacher in school also repeats a lot, doesn't she?"

Sasha agreed but wasn't quite satisfied. "This is a different kind of repeating," he replied. "In school the teacher repeats slogans like 'Russia is great' or

'Socialism is good.' The minister seemed to repeat things because he didn't know what to say."

As if he had read Sasha's mind, Sasha's father suggested that perhaps the minister didn't understand the Bible quite as well as he would like to. "It's difficult to explain to others what you don't understand yourself," he said.

He quickly added, however, that what the minister had said was true. One therefore shouldn't mind hearing it repeated. Didn't the apostle Paul himself say that? Reaching for his Bible, Sasha's father read Philippians 3:1: "I don't mind repeating what I have written before, and you will be safer if I do so."

Sasha's mother stressed what a good man their pastor was. "He's so humble and yet so brave."

They all knew what she meant. Hadn't he spent several years in prison for preaching from the Bible when the government had told him not to? He had preached anyway, so the police had arrested him. But even in prison he had continued preaching about Jesus.

When Sasha was outside playing with his friends, his parents continued the dinner conversation. "Even Sasha is beginning to notice it," his father said.

"And he is only ten years old," his mother added.

They were silent.

"But what can be done about it?" asked her husband. "We have no Bible schools in Russia. There are no Christian books from which to learn. He loves the Lord and he loves the church, but that just isn't enough for a preacher. He means well but needs help. He loves us, too. I'm sure he wants to feed the congregation like a shepherd feeds his flock. Yet how can he without training and help? You know how many passages in the Bible you and I don't understand—and we have as much education as he has."

His wife agreed. At last she said, "If he can't get training, at least he should have some books that explain the Bible. The right kind of books would help him learn how to explain the Bible clearly to the people. Then he wouldn't repeat himself all the time. He would be able to tell us what a Bible passage means."

"And also show us how to apply it to our daily life here in Russia," Sasha's father added.

A Meeting in England

Even as Sasha was asking his questions in Karaganda, Walter Sawatsky and I, together with Archie Goldie of the Baptists, were meeting with several Russians in Brighton, England. Our purpose was to talk about that very problem.

Our Russian friends were saying there weren't enough Bibles in the Soviet Union for all the people, although there were enough for the preachers. At least all their 35,000 evangelical preachers had personal Bibles. They were thankful for that.

Now they had another problem, however. There was nobody to explain the Bible to the preachers. The preachers had no teachers. A few fortunate preachers could take a correspondence course in Moscow. The rest had Bibles but no access to Bible schools or seminaries.

"Do they have other Christian books?" we asked. We knew the answer was "No" before they spoke. The problem seemed so big we just sat there overwhelmed. It seemed impossible to help.

There was no way to bring all those many pastors to our North American Bible schools or seminaries. There was no way our teachers could go to Russia to teach them. There were too many of them. In addition, we didn't know Russian and they didn't know English.

And the government wouldn't allow us to establish a training program anyway. The Russian government was against religion and the church. So training ministers over there or over here just wasn't a good idea, no matter how you looked at it.

There was one solution—to translate a Bible commentary into the Russian language. A Bible commentary explains the whole Bible. If they had these commentary books, the ministers could look up what any part of the Bible meant and explain it to the people in their sermons.

The men from Russia liked the idea. They wanted to start at once. Our friend Alexei Bychkov said enthusiastically, "Let's translate the Bible commentary into Russian!"

Archie Goldie said Baptist World Alliance would give half the money for the project. Walter and I were sure Mennonite Central Committee would give the other half.

"That will be a big help to our preachers. Then they'll understand the Bible and be able to explain it to the people in their preaching and Bible studies," continued Bychkov.

"Which commentary would you like translated?" we asked. "There are so many and not all are equally good or useful."

So we spent two days studying different commentaries. At last the Russians said, "This one!" They had picked William Barclay's *Daily Study Bible*. We supported their choice. They knew their churches and ministers much better than we did.

The Work Begins

We began at once. It was a big job, much bigger than some of us had expected. First we had to get permission to translate the commentary from English into Russian.

The Barclay people said we could use the commentary but asked for $10,000 just for allowing us to translate it. That seemed an awful lot of money, but we had no choice. We paid.

Then we had to find a good translator. It would have to be a person who could read English but whose native language was Russian. We wanted to make sure we got the best translation, not the kind that sounds like a foreigner talking. We wanted it to sound as if William Barclay, who was a Scotsman and wrote in English, had actually been a Russian writing in Russian.

God helped us find the right translator. God led us to Marvin Ziegenhagel, a Russian who had emigrated to Germany. He was well qualified. How thankful we were!

Now the big work of translating 17 books and 5,109 pages could begin. We didn't know when we started that it would take ten years. And we didn't know it would cost so much. But the Mennonites and Baptists worked harmoniously together for a decade. There were many meetings to solve problems and make decisions. We all enjoyed working on this big project.

Once a book was translated, we sent the typed sheets to Russia. If the Russians wanted to make changes, they were free to do so. Sometimes they did, but usually they sent the pages back and said the translation was very good.

Then we sent all the typed pages to a professor of the Russian language in Canada. His job was to check it once more. We wanted him to make sure that the language was the best possible, that the grammar was correct, and that there were no spelling mistakes. Those in Russia had paid attention only to the content, to *what* was translated. The professor in Canada paid attention only to the language, to *how* it was translated.

Then we sent the corrected manuscript to England, where there were skilled people who could get everything ready for the printer. There they made the plates for printing. That's a tricky job because the Russian language doesn't have 26 letters in the alphabet like ours. It has 33. Russian is a beautiful but difficult language.

The English didn't actually print the books. We

sent the plates to Mennonite Publishing House (MPH) in Scottdale, Pennsylvania. There they have all the large printing presses needed for a fine printing job. Finally, when all the pages were printed, MPH made covers and bound everything together into books.

The commentary was ready at last. Hundreds of thousands of words had been faithfully translated. Before becoming finished books, the manuscript had traveled to five different countries—Germany, Russia, Canada, England, and the United States. At least six different people had carefully read it. It had been retyped many times.

The First Book Is Sent to Moscow

The big moment came for sending the first book to the Russian government. A man who heard about this was surprised and asked, "I thought the commentaries were for the ministers. Why did you send them to the government?" He didn't know that the government would have to give permission before the commentaries could be sent to the ministers.

So it was with a special prayer that we sent that very first book to the government in Moscow. Then we waited. Would they give us permission to send many copies to the ministers and churches in their country? Without their permission, we could send no books. We had over 10,000 commentaries ready to ship—but no permission.

The books were stacked in boxes in huge piles in the MPH warehouse in Scottdale. Soon we had 20,000, then 30,000 books, ready to go. Still no permission. Once the government allowed us to send a small quantity—5,000 books, no more. We wanted to send not 5,000 but 50,000. Or more if we got permission. We could only wait—and believe. Believe that God could open the door to Russia.

Now everybody knows a book does no good as long as it sits on the shelf. A book in a box in a dark warehouse does no good either. The only time a book does any good is when somebody picks it up and reads it. But how could the ministers in Russia pick up Barclay's *Daily Study Bible* in a warehouse more than 5,000 miles away? Some people were beginning to wonder if we knew what we were doing.

One man said, "This is foolish. All that work and money was for nothing. You should have made sure you could send the books to Russia *before* you translated and printed them. Now you're stuck with a warehouse full of books and pockets that are empty. The money is gone. Those books won't do anybody any good. Nobody here can read them because they're in Russian."

Was he right? we wondered. Had we acted too quickly? Should we have asked for the permit first? But the officials in the government in Moscow had said, "Show us the book first. How can we say yes or no if we have not read it?"

That made sense. They could only give permission after they knew what was in those commentaries. So we had gone out on a limb. We had acted in faith. We believed if God wanted the ministers in Russia to have these Bible commentaries, God would also open the door for us to ship them in.

People Prayed and Paid

While we waited for the permit, the people in Russia were praying for it. They wanted those Bible helps so badly for themselves, and especially for their ministers, that they started a prayer chain. They prayed without ceasing. When they finished praying for the permit in one church, they started praying for it in another. When they stopped praying in one town, they started praying in another. At all times someone was asking God to move the hearts of those few important men in the Counsel of Religious Affairs empowered to give the permit.

Months and years passed. Still no permit. We too prayed all the time, but we also had more work to do. Not all the 17 books had been translated and printed yet. The project wasn't finished.

While we continued working on it, many people became interested in it. They asked how they could help. We gratefully told them they could help in two ways. They could pray for the permit. And they could give money for the printing. I told the children in one school that we should pray and print. "When we have done that, we should go ahead and print and pray," I said. That became a slogan— "print and pray."

Later, between classes, I overheard a conversation in the hall. One girl asked another which she was going to do, give money to print—or pray? She said she would do both. That was a good answer.

The children in the Locust Grove Mennonite School at Smoketown, Pennsylvania, for example, decided to raise money for printing the Bible commentaries. They thought this would make a good mission project. The general idea of their annual mission project was to show love to other people. Supporting the commentaries fitted in with that.

They announced it early in the year. Some students had already saved their garden-project money from the summer. Others found all kinds of interesting (and sometimes not so interesting) ways to raise money. One girl helped her father with the milking. Another went to market with her mother's shopping list. Other girls did dishes. Some did special household jobs like cleaning windows. A number got babysitting jobs.

Their parents encouraged them. "Keep it up," one mother told a daughter who had helped for a week in the family greenhouse. "The longer you work, the more money your father and I will pay you."

The fellows washed cars on nice days. When the snow came, they shoveled people's driveways. Some gave part of their allowance. They kept thinking of more and more ways to earn money for the commentary project.

Everybody found out about it. The children talked about it in school and at home. They talked about it with the neighbors for whom they did various jobs. Some people were surprised. Why were these children trying to do something like this for the Russians? They weren't at all sure it was a good idea.

"We've studied about Russia in third grade," said one boy. "The Russian people are very nice."

"I really care about the people in Russia," one girl replied to a neighbor woman who didn't approve of the commentaries. "God loves the Russian people," she said. "They need to have Bibles. They need books like these commentaries that explain the Bible."

One skeptical neighbor, who had just finished telling one of the Locust Grove students he was a born-again Christian, was surprised by the boy's reply. "That's great! Then you know why I want to help the Russian people understand the Bible. If they read and understand it, they'll also be converted, like you." The man had nothing to say.

While all this fund-raising was going on, more job opportunities were listed on the bulletin board. Pictures of Russia and its people were put up. Red Russian commentaries were stacked on a table in the hallway. Nearby, a wall-to-ceiling thermometer showed money needed and money raised so far. It all got pretty exciting.

One day they realized they had either set their goal too high or hadn't worked hard enough. They were still short of money. Valentine's Day, the day the project was to stop, was fast approaching. What were they to do?

They had a meeting. It was short and good. "How many of you," a teacher asked, "think we set the goal too high? Raise your hands if you think we should stop now." Not a single hand went up.

"Then what do you suggest?" asked the teacher. "We don't have much time."

Hands instantly went up. The students had talked

among themselves. They knew exactly what they wanted to do. "Our proposal is that this year we buy no Valentine cards. None at all. We give the money we save to the commentary fund."

There was no need to vote. Everybody shouted "Great! Good idea! Let's do it!"

Then came Valentine's Day. As always, they were going to announce in chapel the total amount raised for the mission project. There was a lot of whispering and guessing. How much would it be? Would they reach the goal? Would the thermometer hit the ceiling?

Maribel Kraybill, the principal, addressed them. "You've done a wonderful job raising money for the Russian commentary project," she began. "You've worked hard. You enjoyed it. And your grades haven't suffered one bit because of the time you put into it. All the teachers want me to tell you this. And also that we appreciate so much the good spirit of cooperation."

"When's she going to tell us how much we raised?" a girl whispered to her neighbor. Somebody went "sh-sh-sh."

"You set a high goal for yourselves this year," the principal continued. "You decided to raise $3,000. Now I don't need to tell you that's a lot of money. That's a lot of washing and shoveling, milking and cleaning, gardening and babysitting."

"How much?" one of the boys in the front of the auditorium whispered, loud enough for everyone to hear. Maribel Kraybill also heard it.

"A good question," she replied with a broad

smile. "We all want to know—how much? Did we reach the goal? How much are we short?" She enjoyed playing her stalling game, because she knew they enjoyed the suspense, too.

Then suddenly she held up a three-foot poster. She didn't say a word. This was on the poster: $3,052.00. Applause shook the room. They had done it!

Children in other schools, as well as parents in many churches, were also paying and praying for the commentary project. Many families adopted it as their own private project.

Smuggle Them In

One day a woman came to me and said: "You're wasting your time waiting for the permit. You don't know the Russian government. They'll never give it."

Handing me a paper, she said, "Here, this is how you should do it. It's the only way you'll ever get those Bible helps into Russia." The paper was about smuggling, about taking things like books into another country secretly.

"Forget about the permit and the government," she said. "Just do it!"

We had thought about that but decided against it. We knew that smuggling usually involved lying and deceiving. We didn't want to lie or deceive. We wanted to travel on a straight road, not stumble on a crooked path.

On the other hand, if we *could* smuggle without lying and deceiving, that would be a different matter. We certainly didn't believe Christians should always and in everything obey the government.

When Peter was told to stop preaching about Jesus he replied: "We must obey God rather than men!" We knew there were times we couldn't do what our government asked us to do. When the government said it was alright to keep slaves, some Mennonites and Quakers refused. When the government said Martin Luther King, Jr., couldn't eat in a certain restaurant because he was black, he went right in and sat down. When the British government asked me to become a soldier, I said no—I couldn't kill another person.

Clearly the question wasn't whether or not to obey the Russian government. We couldn't refuse to smuggle commentaries just because the government didn't want the people to have them. The question was whether or not to obey the Bible! The question was whether to speak the truth or lie. What kind of Christian would we be?

I was explaining all this to a man who told me about his experience as a Bible smuggler. He said he took Bibles to Russia all the time without permits. He never told lies. Now that interested me very much. I asked him to explain in more detail.

"Well, it's like this," he began. "We have a camper. It looks normal but is filled with secret compartments. Some secret places are in the walls, some in the floor, some in the ceiling. All are hard to find. Before we go on a trip we fill the secret places with Bibles or other Christian books."

I was going to ask whether that wasn't deceiving,

but he continued. "My wife and two children go along to make it look like we're going on vacation.

"When we get to the Russian border, the customs official asks, 'Do you have any literature and books to declare? Do you have Bibles?' I say no."

"Wait a minute!" I interrupted. "I thought you just told me all the secret compartments in the camper were filled with Bibles and Christian books. How come you said you didn't have any? Wasn't that a fib?"

He laughed again and explained he hadn't told a lie at all. The customs official had asked "Do *you* have any books or Bibles?" He didn't, of course. He didn't have any in his hands or in his pockets. He had none at all. They were in the camper.

"Hold it one moment, please," I interjected. "Suppose he had found those hidden books and Bibles in the secret compartments. Surely then you would have had to admit you had lied."

No, he insisted. Hadn't the customs official asked whether *he* had books or Bibles? Well, these weren't his at all. They belonged to a Bible smuggling agency. They weren't his, nor was the camper. "So you see I didn't tell any fibs," he said.

Another man was more honest. "Yes, of course, I lie," he admitted. "How else can I get the Bibles across the border? If I tell them the truth and show them the Bibles, they'll take them away. What would be the good of trying to take them into the country, then giving them up at the border? That would be foolish."

"What do you mean, foolish?" I asked. "When

you tell the truth, is that foolish? Doesn't the Bible tell us we should speak the truth?"

"Let me explain that," he said. "Of course the Bible tells us to speak the truth. The question is, What does it mean to speak the truth? Do you speak the truth to a burglar who comes into your house to rob you? Do you tell him where your money is? Do you tell him where the keys to your car are? Of course not; that would be foolish. You don't have to tell a robber the truth.

"And you don't have to tell the truth to people who don't believe in God, like the communists. They're liars. They wouldn't know the difference between the truth and a lie. You speak the truth when you talk to Christians but you don't need to speak the truth when you talk to non-Christians. When you don't tell them about the Bibles that you have hidden in the secret compartments of your RV, that's not a lie. A lie is when one Christian speaks an untruth to another Christian."

Wow! I had never heard it explained that way. It sounded wacky to me.

I was deeply disturbed. I didn't know how to reply. Surely he knew that the Bible says, "A poor man is better than a liar" (Proverbs 19:22). And didn't he know what Paul had written to the Colossians? "Don't tell lies to each other; it was your old life with all its wickedness that did that sort of thing; now it is dead and gone." Paul went on to say, "You are living a brand-new kind of life that is continually learning more and more of what is right" (Colossians 3:9).

I was quite sure the Bible didn't support speaking the truth only to Christians and lying to non-Christians. Why do people twist the Bible like that? I wondered.

Christians Are Liars

Suddenly one thing was clear to me. I knew why the Russian customs officials who check travelers' baggage warned, "Watch out for Christians. Nobody lies like a Christian."

The first time I heard that I was shocked. I wanted to protest at once. "It's not true!" I wanted to say, "Christians aren't liars. We speak the truth!" But when I heard this man say that if you lied to a communist customs official it wasn't really a lie, I began to understand.

I could see why so many Christian smugglers lied at the borders. They thought they were just fooling the customs officials; they weren't really lying to them. They meant well. They wanted to take Bibles to people who didn't have any, and that was good. But they didn't realize that when they lied about it they were bad examples of what Christians should be like.

Many of those communist customs officials had never read the Bible. But they were watching how the Christians behaved. Paul once said that many people don't read the Bible; they just "read" the Christians. He said we're like an open letter which people can read. When these customs officials saw that Christians were lying, they didn't say, "Aren't they wonderful people." They said, "Watch out for the Christians!" They said if people who read the Bible go around lying like that, the Bible must be a bad book.

Angels Help Smugglers

Then I read in the paper that an organization in California had found a way to send Bibles to communist countries in their own small airplane. It said angels flew along with the airplane, protecting it and making it invisible. I went to California to talk with these people. They said it was all true. When I asked why their airplane could land without permission, they explained they didn't need permission. Their airplane was invisible. Radar can't detect airplanes accompanied by angels.

That had to be the most bizarre story I'd ever heard. But they insisted they *had*, quite successfully, delivered Christian literature with that airplane. "We went there, unloaded, and came safely back," one of them explained with great satisfaction.

"This is amazing, absolutely amazing," I replied. "Could you tell me more? For example, where did you land in Russia? And how come the Russian customs officials didn't take the Bibles or Christian literature away from you? You didn't have a permit, did you?"

"Of course not. Asking for a permit's a waste of time. They never give permission. This is how we did it." He reached into his drawer, pulled out a clear plastic envelope and handed it to me.

"Here it is. We delivered thousands like this one."

I examined it closely. There were some pages of the Gospel of John in it, a stick of chewing gum, and a drinking straw. It was sealed airtight.

"What's this for?" I asked, holding up the chewing gum.

"That's just so they know who sent it. When they see chewing gum everybody knows it comes from America."

"And what's the purpose of the drinking straw?"

"Ah, now that's a good question. Look carefully. The straw in the plastic envelope holds the two sides apart. Without that there would be no air in it; it wouldn't float. The straw makes an air pocket in the envelope which lets it float in the water."

"Why does it have to float?" I asked. "I thought you said you delivered these packages to Russia."

Excitedly he explained how the airplane had dropped the plastic envelopes with the few pages of the Gospel of John, a stick of chewing gum, and a drinking straw, into the ocean just off the shore of Russia. The plane had taken off from Fairbanks, Alaska, and dumped the plastic envelopes into the Bering Sea. "The Russian shore is right there," he said, laughing and pointing a finger at the map.

I didn't laugh. I didn't think it was funny. And I certainly didn't think what they had printed in their paper about airplanes and angels was honest.

"What happened to the envelopes you dropped in the ocean?" I asked.

"They probably washed ashore," he said. "The people picked them up and read the pages from the Gospel of John."

"How do you know?"

"We don't know for sure," he admitted. "But we think some probably did wash ashore."

"So you have no proof that the Russian people actually got those parts of the Gospel you sent?"

"Well, no, not real proof, but. . . ."

"But it's possible they weren't washed ashore at all? It's possible they were washed out to sea?"

"Yes, I suppose so. But don't you think the straw and chewing gum are a clever idea?"

"Clever, maybe, but what about this article in the paper? It isn't true, is it? The article says the airplane took portions of the Bible INTO a communist country. It didn't take them into a communist country at all. It dumped them into the ocean."

"Ah, well, that's the way you see it," he said. "Look, if we tell our readers everything we do and how we do it, we might as well quit. Smuggling is a complicated business. And quite expensive."

I was sad and disappointed when I left California. It would seem these people had never read what Paul wrote to the Corinthians: "We do not try to trick people into believing—we are not interested in fooling anyone. . . . All such shameful methods we forego . . . we tell the truth" (2 Corinthians 4:2).

I was glad, however, that I had gone to hear and see for myself. Now I knew how these people sent their Bibles to Russia without permission or lying.

I had seen three different ways. I liked none of them. The camper with the secret compartments wasn't honest. Speaking the truth only to Christians but fibbing to non-Christians wasn't honest. And the airplane-and-angels approach certainly wasn't honest. The more I thought about it, the more I seemed to hear God say, "Don't tell lies! Don't try to deceive! Be honest and tell the truth."

Please Don't Hurt Us

There was one more thing we hadn't thought of before. We had thought only of getting the Bible commentaries into Russia. We hadn't thought about how the Christians in Russia would feel if we smuggled the books to them.

The first Russian we asked about this had a surprising answer. "Don't you love us at all? Why do you want to hurt us?" she asked. She explained that the police would make life miserable for any known recipients of smuggled books. But we didn't want to hurt them, we wanted to help.

Now it was clear to us: we couldn't smuggle Bible commentaries into Russia. First, because we weren't going to lie or deceive. And second, because we didn't want to hurt anybody. We had to find an honest way.

The only solution we could think of was to give the first copy of the commentary to the Russian government. We would ask them to read it and request permission to send the other commentaries to the believers in their country. We would, in short, ask for a permit, a license to send commentaries legally. We would do the very thing everyone told us wouldn't work.

We had printed and prayed, prayed and printed,

for almost 10 years. Now the last book was finished. The warehouse at MPH in Scottdale was full. We had taken a leap of faith. When we started we believed God wanted the ministers and people in Russia to have the commentaries. God would also open the door to let them in. We still believed that. Our faith had been severely tested, but it was still strong.

Good News at Last

One day our radios and newspapers reported that Russia had elected a new "president," or General Secretary. His name was Gorbachev. Not long after Mr. Gorbachev was elected, a new word came into the American language. Every reporter used it and all the people in Washington became curious about it. It was the Russian word *glasnost*.

What did it mean? We were told *glasnost* was Gorbachev's idea and meant "openness." Openness to what, we wondered. Until now, the Soviet Union had closed its doors to our commentaries. Would the doors now open? Was that what *glasnost* meant?

We got excited. Was God using the movers and shakers of the world to answer our prayers? If the doors actually opened, the timing couldn't be more perfect. It had taken us exactly ten years to finish the project; exactly when we finished we heard the word *glasnost*, openness, for the first time.

One day we got a telegram. It brought us the welcome news we had been awaiting. *Glasnost did* include our Bible commentaries. The telegram said this: "Send 75,000 commentaries of William Barclay's *Daily Study Bible*. Permission is granted."

Joy filled us. God had answered the prayers of many people. We walked around the house and office all day with smiles on our faces and songs in our hearts. Over and over I repeated, "Thank you, Lord! 'Send 75,000 commentaries.' Thank you, Lord! 'Permission is granted.' Thank you, Lord!"

The rest happened quickly. To move 75,000 books is like moving a small mountain. But the people were willing and the trucks were ready. First MPH workers wrapped the commentaries in watertight cellophane packages. Then they put the packages in sturdy boxes. They picked the boxes up with a forklift and loaded them into huge metal containers for shipping across the ocean. It was an exciting moment. In *Hi-Lights*, their weekly newssheet, MPH reported this:

> THE RUSSIAN COMMENTARIES ARE ON THEIR WAY
>
> The 15-volume, Russian-language Barclay commentary series of the New Testament were loaded in shipping containers . . . and are now on their way to . . . Moscow, USSR. . . . The 5,000 sets of the series, or a total of 75,000 books, were packed in 1,503 cartons and weighed 53,103 pounds. The containers then left for Montreal, Quebec, Canada, where they are scheduled to be loaded on the Russian vessel *Romas*. . . . The containers are due to arrive in Hamburg, Germany, on October 31. From there they will be transported to Moscow by boat, rail, or truck. . . .

So that's the exciting story of the leap of faith. Of God answering prayers! The story of many people creating a Russian-language Bible commentary.

Walter and I were, of course, only two of the many people involved. There was Archie Goldie and his wonderful people at the Baptist World Alliance. There was Alexei Bychkov and his Russian helpers. There was Marvin Ziegenhagel, who had done all the translating. Many more people helped. Some typed the manuscripts. Some corrected them. Others set the type, did the printing, bound the books, and much more.

Helpers included men, women, and yes, the many boys and girls who prayed and gave money. Without the money from the children and churches, without our Baptist helpers and Russian friends, and without countless prayers, this big project would never have been completed. Without God it would have come to nothing!

A Christmas Present

We didn't know how long the commentaries would be on the way. From ship to train to truck could be a long time. Crossing the Russian border might cause the most serious delay. Suppose some official there asked all sorts of questions. "What is a Bible commentary? Who sent those books? Who are they for? Why are there so many?" By the time he got all his answers many weeks and months might pass.

That isn't what happened. With United Bible Society help, the commentaries crossed the border easily, arriving in Moscow sooner than we had expected. Our Russian friends were so happy and thankful they sent us a telegram immediately:

> PRAISE THE LORD! ALL BARCLAY BOOKS REACHED BAPTIST UNION DECEMBER 21. MAY GOD BLESS YOU ALL. MERRY CHRISTMAS, HAPPY NEW YEAR.

The telegram was signed by Logvinenko, president, and Bychkov, general secretary of the All Union Council of Evangelical Christian-Baptists. Next day they sent us another telegram inviting four persons from North America to visit them soon as guests.

The commentaries arrived on December 21, four days before Christmas. Never before had so many ministers in Russia received such a valuable Christmas present. As we sang "Joy to the World" our hearts sang, too. We were thankful and so were they. We were thankful for God's great gift, Jesus Christ. And thankful God had made it possible for the explanation of God's Word, the commentaries, to reach 5,000 ministers in Russia. What an unforgettable Christmas!

More Good News

This could be the end of the story. But it's not. There is more good news. Not long after the Bible commentaries arrived in the Soviet Union, we began to hear about it. A tourist came back from Russia and said, "Everywhere I went, people were talking about the Barclay commentary."

A grandmother wrote to tell us, "God has answered our prayers. Now our pastor has a Bible commentary."

Walter Sawatsky went to Russia and wrote, "The Bible commentary series is widely affirmed."

A pastor from Karaganda wrote me, "I must thank all of you once more for Barclay in the Russian language."

And then came another surprise and challenge. A message from Moscow said, "Please get ready to send us another 75,000 Barclay commentaries." Wow! 75,000 on top of the first 75,000. They were asking for a total of 150,000 commentaries!

That wasn't all. We received word that now the Russian ministers also wanted a commentary to explain the Old Testament. Barclay had explained only the New Testament. What a task! The second job would be even bigger than the first. The New Testament has 27 books—the Old Testament, 39.

The Baptist World Alliance people immediately said they were ready to go ahead with the second and bigger project if Mennonite Central Committee would again cooperate. We said yes, of course we would. With great pleasure.

It will be another leap of faith. But we're confident, especially after our first experience, that God will be with us. Our only concern is to help the ministers in Russia understand the Bible. If they understand it, they can preach from it and teach it. The Spirit of God will do the rest.

Now suppose tourists from North America visited

some Karaganda churches. They would probably meet a number of Mennonite and Baptist ministers. They might also meet Sasha. Sasha and his parents might all be sitting together on the same hard bench in the plain church, singing and praying and listening to the sermon together.

Would Sasha still think the preacher was repeating himself? And if not, why not?

CHAPTER 2

Ouch! That Hurts!

When Pedro awoke the sun was just rising. He glanced at his sleeping wife and one-year-old son. Then he quietly tiptoed from the tiny bedroom.

Like most houses of the poor people in Paraguay, this one had two rooms. One was for sleeping. The other was for everything else—cooking, eating, living, entertaining.

Pedro washed his face in cold water. Briefly he saw himself reflected in the broken mirror on the wall. His eyes were dark, his hair black. If he didn't always dress in old, poor-fitting clothes, he might be considered good looking. Even handsome. But he always wore the same patched pants, and his shirt had long ago lost both sleeves.

Because Pedro was poor and had little education, he had no profession. He had to be content to work for other people, doing whatever they asked him to do. Sometimes he weeded gardens or fixed fences.

Sometimes he helped with the harvest or took care of cows. The little money he earned was just enough to buy food, and the few things he and his wife, Maria, and little son Juan needed.

Pedro was poor but happy. Whenever he thought about Maria and Juan a warm smile came over his light brown face. He loved Maria very much. And he thought there wasn't a more beautiful child in the whole village than his little son Juan. One day he would build a better house for his family. One day he might even have a piece of his own land. Yes, one day he might have his own herd of cows. And why not, one day he might even have his own riding horse. There was nothing wrong with dreaming.

After a quick breakfast of left-over supper and a cup of black coffee, Pedro peeked into the bedroom once more. He whispered a fond "adios" to his sleeping family and left the house.

As he walked down the dusty village street he didn't mind going barefoot. He was used to it. He had no shoes but did own a pair of sandals for church on Sundays. Pedro whistled softly as he walked along with a quick, light step. He greeted his friends and neighbors along the way with a broad smile and a cheerful hello: "Hola!" People liked Pedro and his good wife, Maria.

Suddenly Pedro stepped on a sharp and rusty nail. It pierced the skin of his foot and went into the soft flesh. Pedro didn't stop. His second step drove the nail farther into his foot. Pedro walked on, whistling. He didn't know he had a nail in his foot because he didn't feel any pain. Then the walking worked the nail loose and it dropped off.

A few days later Pedro told Maria he didn't feel so good. She put her hand on his brow. It was hot.

"You have a fever," she told him. "Maybe you're getting a cold."

That day he stayed home, hoping he would feel better in a day or two. Next morning he felt worse. There was nothing to do but stay in bed. Pedro and Maria didn't go to the doctor just because they didn't feel well. They didn't have money for doctor bills and medicine.

Maria was the first to detect a new and unpleasant smell in the house. It was a pungent odor. They didn't know where it came from, but they didn't like it. They wanted to get rid of it. Even when they sat outside the house the smell followed them. Maria looked around carefully for any piece of rotting meat, because that's what it smelled like. Perhaps there was a dead mouse or rat somewhere. She found nothing. They gave up.

Pedro was tired. As he stretched out on his bed Maria reached for the thin blanket at the foot of the bed to cover him up. Suddenly she stopped. She dropped the blanket. She covered her nose. "It's your foot, Pedro!" she exclaimed.

Fortunately, it was not far to Hospital KM 81. They went at once. Dr. Schmidt, a volunteer from Kansas, was in when they arrived. He knew immediately what to do. When the nurses had finished cleaning the wound they brought Pedro back to the doctor. The foul smell was gone. The foot was neatly and professionally bound.

Dr. Schmidt asked Pedro and Maria to sit down and tell them what had happened. "That's our problem," Pedro replied, "we don't know. I must have stepped on a nail. But why didn't I feel it? Why was there no pain?"

Maria told Dr. Schmidt how they had hunted for the foul smell. "If we had known it was his foot we would have done something about it," she explained. "Then all this wouldn't have happened. There would have been no infection and gangrene. Tell us, doctor, is it serious? Is there something wrong with my husband? With more than his foot?"

Kindly and slowly Dr. Schmidt began to explain. "It's your nerves," he said. "The nerve endings in our hands and feet send messages to our brain all the time. That's how we know when we touch something. The nerves in the skin also tell us whether what we're touching is rough or smooth, hot or cold.

"And when something is wrong, like when you put your hand into hot water or step on a nail, the nerves immediately shoot up a message to the brain that says *'Danger!'* As soon as we get that message we cry, 'Ouch! that hurts!' "

Dr. Schmidt paused. He reached down to touch Pedro's toe. "Can you feel that?" he asked.

"No. I can't. I feel nothing."

"That's because your nerve ends don't work, Pedro," explained Dr. Schmidt. "They didn't send the message to the brain now when I touched you. And they didn't send it when you stepped on the nail.

That's why you didn't feel pain."

"I never thought pain was a good thing," Maria said. "I can see I was mistaken. But why didn't Pedro's nerves work?"

"Maybe I can explain that later," Dr. Schmidt answered. "For now let me just say that you, Pedro, have a skin disease. You know, of course, that many people in Paraguay have skin diseases. Here at KM 81 we specialize in looking after people like that."

Dr. Schmidt never told patients directly and bluntly that they had Hansen's disease, which is a form of leprosy. Instead, he would refer them to someone in the area who had Hansen's disease. Then the unsuspecting patients would learn of their own disease slowly, through conversation with their own people. Discovering the disease for themselves lessened the shock.

"I have a suggestion," said Dr. Schmidt. "Before we talk about what you have to do for your foot, and why you didn't feel pain when you stepped on that nail, why don't we go for a little walk. How would you like to visit some of the other patients here in the hospital?

"Most of them have the same problem you have, Pedro. You can observe them and talk with them, too, if you like. Maybe you can learn something that way. You'll notice most of the patients are men. That's because few women get this skin disease. Nine out of ten are men."

The first person they met was a man whose face was strange. He had almost no eyebrows. His nose was like a caved-in bridge. Maria also noticed he had clusters of little lumps or nodules on his ears.

Dr. Schmidt introduced the man to Pedro and Maria. As they reached out to shake hands they noticed his hand was deformed. Some fingers were only stubs; a few were missing altogether. For a moment they wondered whether they should shake his hand. Perhaps by touching him they would also get his terrible disease.

It hadn't occurred to Pedro yet that he already had the same sickness. Maria certainly had no idea that what had happened to this man was the same thing that had happened to her Pedro. But they both had seen people with leprosy before and thought this man was a leprosy patient.

"Dr. Schmidt, what was wrong with that man?" Pedro asked as they walked away from him."

"He has Hansen's disease," the doctor replied. Pedro and Maria looked at each other. Their eyes grew bigger. Maria was about to cry when Pedro put his arms around her and said reassuringly, "No, no, Maria, I am not like that! It's just that my foot . . . I mean, I didn't feel the pain . . . I mean. . . ."

Pedro and Maria turned to Dr. Schmidt. They had many questions—but one in particular. They hesitated to ask it. And it was Dr. Schmidt's conviction that he should not tell them until they had discovered it for themselves. There was a long silence while they groped for the right words. And the courage to speak them.

It was Pedro who finally said, "Dr. Schmidt, it seems to me I have the same skin disease these people have. I think I am leprous like they."

Dr. Schmidt took their hands in his. He looked deep into their puzzled and frightened eyes. Then he said, in as kind a voice as he could, "Pedro, you're right. You do have Hansen's disease."

There was a bench along the path. The doctor asked them to sit down. For a moment there was nothing more to say; they both needed time to get over the shock.

When Maria had dried her eyes and both had turned to Dr. Schmidt again, he continued. "The man we saw back there came to the hospital too late. Too late to save his hands, but not too late to get help. It's a good thing you came when you did, Pedro and Maria. I hope we can save your foot."

They both heard the doctor but still didn't fully understand what he meant. They walked on and came to a room that looked like a shoemaker's workshop. There were shoes of every shape, size, and description on the shelves. Two men were sitting at their machines with half-finished shoes before them. The air was filled with the smell of leather. Pedro and Maria had no idea what this was all about. Why would a hospital employ shoemakers? Surely hospitals employ doctors and nurses, not shoemakers.

Dr. Schmidt could see they were puzzled. He reached for a pair of shoes on the shelf. "Look at this shoe," he said. "It's not for a normal foot. See how short and stubby it is? It's for a man who has no toes. And see this one, it's for a man who lost even more than his toes. Every year these two shoemakers make almost 500 pair of special shoes for patients who can't wear normal shoes anymore.

"Pedro, you're very fortunate you came here today. I'll do everything I can to save your foot."

As they left the strange cobbler workshop, Pedro noticed crutches hanging from the ceiling. Maria nudged him to look at the many different artificial legs leaning against the wall. They were made of wood.

Seeing what they were looking at, the doctor explained: "Unfortunately, some people with Hansen's disease come to us too late. We can't save their feet or legs anymore, but we can still help them with those prostheses, or artificial limbs."

Back in the office Dr. Schmidt asked them to sit down once more. He knew Pedro and Maria had a lot of questions.

"Let me tell you something about Hansen's disease before we talk about your foot," he began. "It's a very old disease. It has been around for thousands of years. Perhaps you remember the story about Lazarus in the Bible? He had that dreaded skin disease. Or the story about the ten lepers that Jesus healed?"

Pedro and Maria nodded. Yes, they knew these stories. The ten men were outcasts. They lived in caves, because people were afraid that if they came close to them they would also get the disease.

Pedro and Maria remembered that these unfortunate people, whom the Bible simply calls "lepers," had to shout, "Unclean, unclean!" whenever people came close. Then Jesus healed ten of them. But only one had gone back to thank Jesus.

From the way they told the story, Dr. Schmidt could tell Pedro and Maria were churchgoing people. They knew the Bible.

"Now that was long ago," he continued. "People then didn't know much about the disease. They didn't know what caused it nor how it was spread."

He moved over to a microscope and continued. "Today we know it's caused by a bacterium. This is a very tiny organism you can't see with your naked eye. When it's enlarged it looks like a straight or slightly curved rod or stick. Would you like to see these bacteria?" he asked.

Dr. Schmidt showed them how to look into the microscope. "Now look carefully for those tiny rods or sticks. Often they cluster together, so look for a tiny bundle of sticks. Can you see them?"

Pedro and Maria looked through the microscope. It was the first time they had ever done that. They both saw the bacteria. They were fascinated. Maria saw some that were slightly curved. Pedro thought the ones he saw looked like a bunch of matches.

Dr. Schmidt explained that the bacillus or bacteria they were seeing through the microscope, which looked like harmless little sticks, were the mischief-makers that had affected the nerve endings of Pedro's foot. They were, in fact, not much different from the bacilli that cause tuberculosis, the sickness that often affects people's lungs.

"Did Pedro get that sickness from his parents?" Maria asked. "And have we already passed it on to our little son, Juan?"

"No, Pedro didn't inherit the disease from his

parents. And you didn't pass it to your son," Dr. Schmidt explained. "Those powerful little sticks, which we doctors have given the big name of 'mycobacterium leprae,' can't be passed on like that. The disease isn't inherited. People used to think it was transmitted from parents to children, but that's not true.

"They also used to think another person could get the disease just by coming too close to a leprosy patient. That's why, long ago, they made the law that people with leprosy had to stay far away from other people. That's why people with leprosy had to call out to all who came their way, 'unclean, unclean.' But you don't get the disease that way either. Come outside again, I'd like to show you something."

Pedro and Maria followed Dr. Schmidt outside. "Do you see those tall eucalyptus trees?" he asked, pointing to seven or eight long rows of trees reaching into the sky.

"We planted those trees long ago, when we started this hospital. At that time, we also thought the bacteria that cause leprosy might be carried from one person to another by the wind. On this side of the trees we used to treat normal patients, people with all kinds of ordinary sicknesses, but not leprosy patients. Women came here to the hospital to have their babies, for example.

"On the other side of the trees we treated only leprosy patients. We planted those trees between the two parts of the hospital to protect the patients on this side from the leprosy patients on the other side. Not from the people, of course, but from the bacteria. We thought perhaps the trees would catch the bacteria floating in the breeze and stop it from reaching this side. Today we know that was a lot of nonsense. It wasn't very scientific."

Dr. Schmidt laughed as he stood there looking at those hundreds of trees. Then he added: "But they look nice, don't you think?"

"If the disease isn't inherited from parents or sent through the air, how does it pass from one person to another?" Pedro asked. "Why is it that often more than one person in the same family has it, while other families don't have it? It would seem that being close together does have something to do with passing it on."

"That's a very good observation, Pedro," replied Dr. Schmidt. "They used to think that the disease was transmitted primarily through direct and prolonged skin contact. Like an African leprous mother transmitting the disease to her child by carrying it on her back or hip for a long time."

He paused and reached for a medical book. Then he put it down again, unopened. "Today we don't believe so much in the direct skin contact theory," he explained.

"You must both pay close attention to what I'm going to say now, because it affects the future of your little son. Let me say it as clearly and briefly as I can. Doctors today believe the disease is passed from one person to another very much the way tuberculosis is passed on—*through the nose*."

"Through the nose!" Pedro and Maria echoed in surprise. "Why?"

"We don't understand it all ourselves yet," confessed Dr. Schmidt, "but we do know the best way to stop the disease from spreading is through cleanliness. Keep your house and clothes, your towels and linens, spotless. Take your medicine. And, of course, you must return to the hospital regularly."

Pedro and Maria had listened attentively. They thought they understood what Dr. Schmidt was saying. Still they had one unanswered question: would Pedro ever be completely healed?

"I certainly hope so," replied the doctor with a broad smile. "Today we know enough about Hansen's disease to cure the patient. Provided, of course, that you follow our instructions. In fact, we hope to see Paraguay free of leprosy one day."

"And now, Pedro, we're going to examine you very thoroughly, every part of your body. So far we've only treated your foot. Let's see if you have more dead nerve endings. Let me see your hands."

As he examined Pedro's hands, Dr. Schmidt went on to say that the disease could be in any part of the body but the most common places to find it were in the "cold" parts of the skin, like earlobes, fingers, and toes.

"Maria, keep looking for red or white spots on Pedro's body," the doctor advised. "If you see spots or blotches on the skin that are either red or white, test whether he has any feeling in them. Just stick a pin in them. If he says, 'Ouch, that hurts!' you don't need to worry. But if he doesn't feel anything, be sure to send him to me at once."

Back home, Pedro and Maria were quiet a long

time. They had so much to think about. Maria stood by the simple wood stove stirring the rice they were going to eat for dinner. Pedro held Juan on his knees. He wanted to hug his boy but didn't know if he should. What did the doctor mean, the disease spread through the nose?

Finally, Maria broke the silence and said, "I have lived 24 years, and I have never heard that pain is a good thing! Today I heard it for the first time. Today I saw for the first time with my own eyes what terrible things happen when a person doesn't feel pain. Pedro, do you remember that man without fingers?"

"Yes, Maria. And I also remember how I felt about shaking hands with those little stubs that were left where the fingers once had been. Maria, do you remember all those strangely shaped shoes? To think that they make almost 500 pairs a year like that! I wonder how many people with leprosy there are in Paraguay?"

"Don't you remember? The doctor told us there were 15,000," Maria reminded him.

She almost added, "Well, now we know there's one more."

But she didn't. It would have been unkind. Pedro was hurting enough as it was. Now she knew there was a physical pain that was good, but now she also felt there was another kind of pain that was not good. Why should she say something that might hurt Pedro when she loved him dearly?

And suddenly Maria found herself thinking more new thoughts. Thoughts about good pain and bad pain. She had never thought about that before. If Pedro had felt the pain in his foot when he stepped on the nail that would have been a good pain. But if she said something unkind that would hurt him, that would be a bad pain. She wondered if she was right about that. Could she discuss this with someone else? Perhaps her pastor?

Next Sunday Pedro put on his sandals and they all went to church, even little Juan. Pedro and Maria loved the church. On this Sunday they felt particularly happy about going because of the experience with Pedro's foot. They wanted to thank God in church, as they had already thanked him at home. They wanted to thank God that the disease had been discovered before it was too late.

After the singing and prayer, the pastor announced he was going to preach on the value of having a conscience. Maria thought this would be either a dull sermon or one she wouldn't understand. She was mistaken. She didn't know she was going to have a surprise.

"You know what a conscience is," the pastor began. "It's that little voice inside us that tells us what's right and what's wrong. The apostle Paul wrote a letter to the Romans in which he said everybody has a conscience. He said it tells people what's true and what's false, "since their thoughts sometimes accuse them and sometimes defend them" (Romans 2:15).

Another time Paul boasted, "My conscience is perfectly clear about the way in which I have lived before God to this very day" (Acts 23:1).

Then came the surprise. The pastor said he was going to talk about how wonderful it was to have a bad conscience. Maria didn't think she had heard right. How could a bad conscience be wonderful?

"Paul had a good conscience," the preacher went on. "That's why he wrote, 'my conscience is perfectly clear.' But we all know Paul had done terrible things. He persecuted Christians. He arrested them and had them thrown into jail. On one occasion he watched the stoning of a believer named Stephen. They killed him and Paul was happy about it. He watched that nobody stole the clothes of the people who threw the stones.

"Now how could Paul say, 'My conscience is perfectly clear'? Shouldn't he have said, 'I have a guilty conscience? I did a terrible thing'?"

The pastor added that some people came to church hoping he would say nothing to make them feel guilty and give them a bad conscience. "Don't send us on a guilt trip," someone had told him.

Another person had said, "Pastor, we don't want to hear about the poor people in the world. That makes us feel guilty. If you tell us we're rich and they're poor, and that we don't share with them, look what you've done. Made us all miserable. The poor because they have nothing—and we because we have a guilty conscience and can't even enjoy our wealth."

Still another person had come to the pastor and asked him not to preach about loving everybody. "You know, pastor, how impossible that is. If we loved everybody, we'd have to love the Russians.

We can't do that. The Russians are communists. They're our enemies. One doesn't love an enemy."

"So I asked that person, 'What should I do with Jesus?' I reminded him that Jesus told us to love our enemies.

" 'That's your problem,' he replied. 'But you have no right to make us feel guilty. You're supposed to encourage and comfort us.'

"Some people don't want to be told not to smoke and drink. When they do it anyway, it just makes them feel guilty. Young people don't want to be told not to use drugs. When they do it anyway, they remember what the preacher said. It just makes them feel guilty. Nobody wants to feel guilty.

"That's why people say, 'Don't send us on a guilt trip. It just makes us feel bad.'

"And you know what? They're right. I agree one hundred percent. People shouldn't go around feeling guilty all the time. That's even bad for your health. It could warp your personality and character. I say, get rid of guilt."

Maria and Pedro weren't sure they understood right. First he seemed to say it was alright to feel guilty. Now he was saying get rid of guilt feelings.

The pastor went on. "Guilt feelings are like a smoke-detector in your house. As soon as it goes off, you run to turn it off. Nobody wants to listen to a smoke-detector screaming. But it told you there was a fire and saved your house. It made you get out of bed quickly and put out the fire.

"Guilt feelings are like a nail in the foot. As soon

as you feel the nail you pull it out. But without the pain you wouldn't have found out you had a nail in your foot. The pain saved your foot from getting infected and perhaps having to be amputated.

"So what's wrong with feeling guilty?" the pastor asked. "You might as well ask, 'What's wrong with having a conscience?'

"Suppose you had no conscience. Suppose nothing inside you told you when you were doing right or wrong. Wouldn't that be the same as having no feeling in your hands or feet? You wouldn't be able tell when you hurt yourself!"

Maria sat up straight and listened. Not only could she understand every word the preacher was saying, she also knew he was absolutely right. A week ago she wouldn't have understood nearly as well as she did now.

"Have you ever seen a person with leprosy?" the pastor asked. Pedro shifted uneasily beside her, Maria noticed.

"Have you seen their deformed and crippled hands and feet?

"Do you know what happened? It's simple to explain. It's as if the brain had said, 'Don't send me any pain messages. Don't send me on a pain trip.'

"The nerves obeyed. They sent no pain message when the man put his hand in boiling water. He didn't feel the heat. So his hand got badly scalded. He lost his fingers.

"The nerves in the foot didn't send a pain message when the man stepped on a nail. The foot festered, then gangrene set in. He lost all his toes. If only the nerves had sent pain messages. Then the man would have known something was wrong and done something about it.

"Our conscience sends pain messages. When we've done wrong, it says, 'Danger! Do something!'

"Sometimes our conscience accuses us, 'That wasn't very kind, what you just did.' Sometimes the little voice inside us whispers, 'That wasn't true, what you just said.' Then we should be thankful for the warning. Now we can make things right.

"How do you think Paul felt after he found out what he had done was wrong? Terrible. Miserable. For days he couldn't eat, sleep, or talk to anyone. He wished he could die. Finally he broke down. He confessed to God and the church what a terrible thing he had done.

"Then God forgave Paul everything. God took all his guilt and sin away, giving him a clean conscience, making him a happy man.

"That couldn't have happened if his conscience hadn't sent a message saying, 'Danger! You did wrong! Make it right or I'll keep bothering you!' "

The pastor closed his message saying, "So the next time you see a leprous person with deformed hands and feet, or a caved-in nose, just think how fortunate you are that your nerve endings work.

"When you cut yourself, you feel pain. When you step on a rusty nail, you cry out, 'Ouch!' It's wonderful to feel pain!

"My friends, next time your conscience bothers you, or the little voice inside of you whispers or screams, 'Danger!' listen—and be thankful."

Maria and Pedro had never heard a sermon quite like that before. Afterward their pastor prayed, thanking God for the capacity to feel both physical and spiritual pain. He thanked God for the pain in our bodies and the pain of a guilty conscience. Both signaled something was wrong. Both demanded immediate attention and action.

The worse thing you could have was a conscience that didn't bother you at all. Then you had spiritual leprosy. For a while it might be wonderful to feel no pain, but then would come disaster.

Maria and Pedro couldn't help thinking how strangely yet how wonderfully everything was coming together for them.

The next week Pedro went back to Dr. Schmidt. As he came to KM 81 he noticed the large sign by the road which read: "HOSPITAL MENONITA." He hadn't seen that the first time. When Dr. Schmidt received him, Pedro asked what the sign meant. He knew what the word "hospital" meant but not the other word, "Menonita."

The doctor sat back and smiled. "That's a long story," he began, "but I'll tell it in very few words. It has to do with gratitude, with being thankful. It has to do with my people, the Mennonites, and your people, the Paraguayans.

"You see, Pedro, about 40 years ago the Mennonites in Russia had a rough time. They lost their possessions and their freedom. Hardest of all was losing their right to worship God the way they had been used to. So they wanted to leave Russia. But where should they go? They knocked on the doors of many countries. All said no.

"Finally, Paraguay said they were welcome to come and settle in this country. The Mennonites did. It was difficult at first, but they were grateful to be free. They worked hard. They built schools and hospitals. They built roads and factories. They helped the Indians.

"One day they had an idea. It was a bold and brave idea. It was a new and good idea. They would say 'thank you' to Paraguay for letting them come and settle here. Especially when nobody else would take them. They had many meetings about the best way to say 'thank you.' Some thought they should build a large stone monument. Others thought they should write a book about it.

"Then someone suggested a hospital for the many people in the country with leprosy. Everybody liked that. It was the best idea. They talked with the government and the doctors in Paraguay. Everybody agreed it was a splendid idea. To heal the people who had Hansen's disease, they said, is the best way to say a big 'THANK YOU!'

"So we built this 'Hospital Menonita.' And because it's exactly 81 kilometers from Asuncion, the capital of Paraguay, everybody just talks about KM 81. They all know what that means."

Pedro had never heard that before. He thought it was an exciting story and wanted to remember it all so he could tell it to Maria when he got home. Then he noticed other patients waiting outside and asked Dr. Schmidt whether they were all leprous patients coming to see him.

"Some are. Many aren't," replied Dr. Schmidt. "And they haven't all come to see me. We have four doctors here, but even that isn't enough.

"Last year we treated 1,261 patients with leprosy. We did 320 operations. We had 80 babies born here. We made over 1,600 house calls. We have 40 beds for patients with leprosy and 25 beds for other patients. The nurses are very busy but we also have a lot of volunteers."

"What are volunteers?" Pedro asked. "Who are they and why do they come to work here?"

"A volunteer is a person who works here without getting paid," Dr. Schmidt explained. "They come from the Mennonite colonies. They come for as long as they can, some for a few months, but many for a year or longer. They do it as their way of saying 'Thank you' to Paraguay.

"They also do it because they want to help the people get well again. And because they love Jesus. They want to follow the example of Jesus in serving and healing."

Dr. Schmidt leaned forward and said, "Pedro, that may all be very interesting. But you haven't shown me your foot. How is it? Let's see it."

After a careful examination and more instructions, Pedro promised to come again in another month. The wound was healing very nicely. He was especially thankful that the doctor was sure the medication was helping him with his bigger problem, Hansen's disease.

"We're going to lick that one, too!" Dr. Schmidt promised, just as two jeeps drove up.

Pedro turned to watch three people climb out of each jeep and enter the clinic. Dr. Schmidt knew Pedro was a curious person who wanted to know as much as possible about what was going on. "Would you like to know who they are and where they came from?" he asked. Pedro nodded.

"The three persons in each jeep work as a team," Dr. Schmidt began. "One is a doctor, another is a pastor, and the third is the record keeper and driver. They visit the leprous patients who forget to come back to the hospital when they're supposed to. Last year they were on the road for 134 days and drove more than 25,000 miles. They just came back now from one of those trips."

Then, half joking and half serious, he continued. "And if you don't come back, Pedro, when you're supposed to come, one of those jeeps with three people in it is going to come to *your* house!"

They both laughed as they shook hands and Pedro reached for the door. "And give my greetings to Maria," Dr. Schmidt called after him.

So much had happened to Pedro in the past two weeks. As he walked home along the familiar dusty road he remembered the rusty nail. He remembered the bad smell of his foot. Yes, and he remembered the shock when he first heard he had Hansen's disease. He remembered learning that new word. And he remembered the rows of shoes for deformed feet, and the crutches.

He also remembered the pastor's sermon about thanking God for pain and for a guilty conscience. He thought about the Mennonites coming to Paraguay and starting this hospital. About the volunteers. And so much more.

As Pedro walked along the village street in pants that were too short for him and a shirt that had no sleeves, his heart was singing with praise and thanksgiving. Wasn't he the luckiest man in the whole world? he thought. He had a wonderful wife, Maria. They had their lovely boy, Juan. They had their own two-room house. They had lots of friends. And now they had a new friend, Dr. Schmidt.

Yes, he had Hansen's disease. But his foot was healing and the doctor had said that one day he would be cured of "that dreaded disease."

As Pedro came closer to his house he could see Maria and Juan waiting for him beside the open door. She would have beans and rice ready for supper. He wanted to rush forward and scoop them up in his arms—but he didn't. He wasn't quite finished with his last thought.

Pedro was thinking this: What if, one day—after he was healed—he went back to Dr. Schmidt and the Mennonites to offer himself as a hospital volunteer? Maybe Maria could volunteer, too. What would they say? Would they accept?

It would be the perfect way to thank Dr. Schmidt and all the people at KM 81. And God.

CHAPTER 3

What's in a Name?

*M*y name is Peter. I like my name. I've heard it spoken in many languages. It seems that in all of them it starts with a "P." I like the Spanish sound of *Pedro*. In Greek it is *Petros*, which means rock. A rock in Greek is a *petra*.

Peter seems to be the kind of name that has always been around. But it hasn't. In the long history of the Jews, there is nobody with that name. It isn't mentioned once in the Old Testament.

One day Jesus conducted a sort of opinion poll. He asked his disciples what people were saying about him. Who did the people say he really was?

"Some say you are John the Baptist," they replied. That was an interesting answer because everybody knew John the Baptist had been killed about a year before. He was dead. So what did they think—that he was alive again?

"Others say you are the prophet Elijah," they

added. That was even stranger. Elijah had died about 800 years before. He had been a great prophet. But that was long ago. How could the people be so confused as to think Jesus was Elijah?

"What about you?" Jesus asked his disciples. "Who do you say I am?"

Now among the twelve disciples there was a fisherman. His name was Simon. In those days people had only one name. They were called John or James, Mary or Martha, but had no family names. There were a lot of people with the same names, of course. One way of keeping them apart was by saying that so-and-so was the son of such-and-such a man. Simon, the fisherman, for example, was the son of John.

So when Jesus asked his disciples who they thought he was, Simon answered: "You are the Messiah, the Son of the living God." Maybe that's what the other eleven were going to say too; we don't know. Simon, always quick, said it first. When Jesus heard, he was pleased. He was impressed.

"Good for you, Simon son of John!" answered Jesus. He called him by his full name, so to speak.

Then Jesus continued. "I tell you, Simon son of John, you are a rock and *Petros* [rock] shall be your name."

From then on Simon was his old name, which hardly anybody used. His new name was Petros, or Peter. So the fisherman got a new name. And he also became a new person. He became a Christian. Of course Peter continued fishing, but most of the time he didn't fish for fish as much as for people.

Peter fished for people who were unhappy. He fished for people whose lives were falling apart. People who had really messed things up. He brought them to Jesus. There they became happy again. They became, like Peter, new persons. They also became Christians.

Now some people believe that a name is just a name, nothing more and nothing less. It's a tag, a way of telling one person apart from another. Even the great William Shakespeare said in his play *Romeo and Juliet*:

> What's in a name?
> That which we call a rose
> by any other name
> would smell as sweet.

Shakespeare is right, of course. If you called a rose a stinkweed, it wouldn't stink. It would still smell as sweet as a rose. Yet to say that a name is nothing more than a device to tell people apart isn't true. Then we might as well give everybody a number. To number our children instead of naming them would be to miss the point. They aren't statistics, to be numbered, but people. They're human, unique, as different as our fingerprints.

Peter isn't the only one who got his name in an interesting way—and because of meaning. Elfrieda, my wife, did too. In Peter's case, there was what is called a play on words. Jesus said, "I tell you, Peter; you are a rock [a petros], and on this rock I will build my church."

In Elfrieda's case, there was also a play on words. It happened this way.

It was the year 1917 in Russia. World War I was in its third year. The Mennonites refused to participate in the war. As many as 12,000 young men were doing some other kind of service for the country instead of fighting. About half of them did medical work and the other half worked in forests. Among those working in the forests were about five or six Klassen brothers.

One day these brothers got a telegram from home. This is what their parents said in the telegram: "You have a new baby sister. We want you to pick a name for her."

The brothers were surprised and happy. They celebrated their baby sister's arrival with a song. After the song they laughed and joked around. She was the fourteenth child in the family. They wondered what she looked like. And they wondered how long it would be until they could go home and see her.

They were so tired of the war and the work in the forest. So tired of living in makeshift barracks instead of homes. Tired of the same kind of food every day. Tired of living with hundreds of men and never seeing a girl, their sister or mother. Tired of the meetings, even the meetings for Sunday morning worship.

They wanted to go home. To eat mother's cooking. To hear a sermon from their own preacher in their home church.

"Hey, fellows," said Cornelius, the oldest of the

boys, "let's not forget the second part of the telegram."

"Read it again," said Frank, the second oldest. "Let's make sure we understand what our parents want us to do."

Cornelius read again, "We want you to pick a name for her."

"We've already got Justina and Agatha," said Jake. "This one had better be good."

The brothers turned serious and quiet, thinking. Finally Henry asked, "What is it, at this time, that we want more than anything else?"

He didn't have to wait long for an answer. Everybody said, "Peace. We want peace. We want this awful war to end."

Now the brothers were talking German, the language they usually spoke among themselves and at home. So the word they had used for peace was *Friede*.

"Let's name her "Frieda," they said. "Peace."

"How about going one better?" asked Cornelius. "I don't know much Hebrew, but I think one of the words for God in Hebrew is *El*. Doesn't Beth*el* mean 'house of God?' "

"A brilliant idea," agreed Henry. "Let's name her *El*frieda, the God of peace."

"I don't know how brilliant that is," replied Jake, "stringing a Hebrew and a German word together, but I like it."

They all liked it. The next day the Klassen brothers sent a telegram to their parents saying, "Her name shall be Elfrieda." And that's how my wife got her name.

One day Elfrieda (God of Peace) and I were to be taken to a railroad station somewhere in Virginia. We had just finished the evening meeting. We had told about the refugees Mennonite Central Committee had asked us to take to South America. Now we were to travel to another church.

A friendly couple greeted us and said they were going to take us to the train. It was late in the evening, and dark. We climbed into their car. It was big. Soon we discovered why—they had a lot of children. A little like Elfrieda's family, the Klassens. At least four sat with Elfrieda and me in the back seat. Any number of them were with their parents in the front seat. It was too dark to count them all, but we noticed that the mother held a baby in her arms. The father drove.

Soon after we had left town and were on the open road, the mother introduced the children to us. She began with the oldest boy in the back seat and the girl sitting between us. Then she named another one. Neither Elfrieda nor I could tell from the sound of the name whether it was a boy or a girl. Another name followed, and another. Almost as soon as we heard a name, we forgot it. They were so unusual.

Then she said that the boy on my lap was James and the girl on Elfrieda's lap was Mary. The baby on her own lap was named Elizabeth. I believe there was also a Peter and a Martha in the car.

We said we were pleased to meet all the children. Then we mentioned that the last names had seemed rather different from the first ones. We didn't say whether we liked them better or not—we didn't want to offend the parents. We just said the names were different.

Both parents were pleased we had noticed that. In fact, they seemed eager to talk about it. It was an interesting story that we heard that night in that crowded car on the way to a railroad station somewhere in Virginia.

It was a story about two young people falling in love. A story about getting married and having children. A story about not knowing God and having no relationship to Jesus Christ. A story about never going to church, never reading the Bible or praying. They were not Christians.

They lived like that for many years. They were neither unhappy nor happy. He had a good job, they were healthy, life rolled along. They didn't think much about what they wanted to do with their lives. They just drifted through their days. And had one child after the other. Five, to be exact.

Then came the big event. The thing that changed everything.

"You tell about it," said the husband to his wife. "Tell Peter and Elfrieda how we got turned around."

The good woman told how they had been introduced to Jesus. How they had said yes to him. How they had become his disciples, like that fisherman long ago, Simon the son of John. From then on their lives were filled with new meaning. There was forgiveness and joy. For the first time they experienced what really living meant. All their values changed. When she began talking about their values she paused a bit. We heard the husband chuckling behind the wheel.

"You better believe it, our values changed," he commented. "Tell them about the naming of our children."

She told us how they had picked a name for their first child out of a book. Just any name. The important thing was that it was different. They did the same thing with the second and third child. With the fourth one they played around with different sounds, just making up nonsensical words. It was a game. When they hit on one that sounded really different from any name they had ever heard they decided that was good enough.

Then they became Christians. She was pregnant again. They talked about a name for the unborn child. Both agreed they wouldn't pick meaningless names anymore. The baby was a girl. They named her Martha, after the good friend of Jesus. The next baby was a boy. They named him James, after the brother of Jesus. There's a little book or letter by him in the Bible. The last baby, the one on her mother's lap, was Elizabeth, obviously named after the mother of John the Baptist. They were all New Testament names.

Long after we had said good-bye to these fine people and all their wonderful children, the ones with the strange and the ones with the not-so-strange names, we were still talking about them. Long after we had boarded the train and spoken at another meeting we remembered those people. We could not easily forget them and that unusual conversation in their car.

We had seen other people change. We knew of an alcoholic who stopped drinking when he said yes to Jesus. We knew of a rich and stingy man who became generous when he became a Christian. He enjoyed sharing his money with others, especially the poor. We had seen many people change, some more, some less, after they had made a deliberate decision to follow Jesus.

We had never met anyone whose change had been so complete that it included even the naming of their children. I suppose if we had asked them, "What's in a name?" they might have chuckled and replied, "Do you want to hear our 'before' and 'after' story again?"

CHAPTER 4

The Way of Peace

*H*is name is Samuel but everybody calls him Sami. Sami Gerber lives in Switzerland. He is my friend. One day we had a long and intense discussion about peace. "Can a Christian be a soldier?" I asked.

"Not in America," Sami replied, "but it's different in Switzerland. In America you have to refuse military service if you want to follow Jesus. In Switzerland you can put on the uniform, join the army, and still follow Jesus."

"I never heard of such a thing in my life," I replied. "How can it be right to be a soldier in Switzerland but wrong to be a soldier in America? Soldiering is the same in the whole world, including Switzerland. A soldier's job is to fight and if necessary to kill."

"Not true," my good friend Sami replied. "Let me explain the difference between an American and a Swiss soldier. Your soldiers are sent to all parts of the world. Ours stay at home. They never leave Switzerland. That's one big difference.

"The other is that your soldiers fight aggressive wars. You attack. We don't. We only fight defensive wars. We never attack anybody. We only defend ourselves when somebody else attacks us."

"Look at our history," Sami continued. "You can go back hundreds of years and you won't find a single battle where the Swiss soldiers left Switzerland to attack another country. Not even in the two big wars, World War I and World War II.

"But American soldiers are always fighting abroad—in Europe and Korea, in Africa and Vietnam. American soldiers fought in both World Wars. And in many other wars."

Sami was right, of course. But I wasn't satisfied with his answer. It still seemed to me that soldiering is the same whether you fight at home or abroad, whether you fight to attack or to defend. Americans always say they're defending something when they fight abroad. Either they're defending the Korean people or freedom and democracy in Vietnam. They always seem to be defending religion and the church.

So I turned to Sami once more and asked, "If a soldier's job is to fight and if necessary to kill, how can it be unchristian when an American soldier does it, but Christian when a Swiss soldier does it? Does defending and attacking really make all the difference?"

"Let me explain one more thing," Sami said.

"Many of us in the Swiss army are in a special part of the army called the 'Medics.' We're not trained to fight. We would never kill. We give first aid to the wounded soldiers. We save lives. That makes all the difference."

Sami smiled and sat back. He seemed to think he had now given me a final explanation of why it was okay for a Christian to be in the Swiss army but not in the American army. "We medics never take another person's life, we save life," he repeated.

Now I had to agree that being in the medical part of the army was different from being in the fighting part. But I was still puzzled. The medics were *in* the army exactly like any other soldier. They wore the army uniform. The army paid them. They had to obey army commands.

How could I explain to Sami that I thought that just being *in* the army was wrong? No matter what your job in the army happened to be, it was wrong. For example, a lot of different people are needed to run an army. Not all of them shoot and drop bombs. Some drive trucks and jeeps. Others cook the meals and do the laundry. Still others are in radio communication. And some do medical work.

But no matter what their particular job happens to be, they all work together as a team. They all help fight the enemy. All, directly and indirectly, kill other people. That's what armies do. And that's wrong. That isn't Christian. Violence isn't the Jesus way of solving problems.

"Let me tell you a story," I began. "Perhaps this will explain better than I have so far why I think just being *in* the army is wrong. It doesn't matter what your job in the army is, being in the army is what's unchristian."

Sami told me to go ahead. He was a good listener. I like him even when we don't agree. He told me he did his military service as a Medic every year and it didn't bother him at all. It would bother him if he didn't do it, in fact. So I told my story.

Once there were ten men who agreed to rob a bank. They had carefully worked out a plan. Every man knew exactly what to do. One was to drive the van. Another was to break into the building. A third was to crack the safe. Two were to put the money in bags. Two were to stand watch.

Now there was one man in the group who had refused to have anything to do with the robbery. He didn't think it was right. But they were all friends and the others insisted he come along. Then they had an idea.

They thought it was a brilliant idea. He wouldn't need to break down the door or crack the safe. He wouldn't need to be a lookout or scoop up the money. All he would need to do was carry a first-aid kit. After all, something might go wrong and somebody might get hurt. And wasn't he a medic? In that way he wouldn't be a part of the robbery at all. He would be there to help and to heal in case somebody got hurt.

The medic liked the idea. So he took his first-aid kit and went along. But something went wrong. Suddenly there was a bright light. Police surrounded them. The police took them to prison and then to court.

In court, facing the judge, the man with the first-aid kit pleaded "not guilty." Yes, he had been caught along with the others, he admitted. The other men might have been caught red-handed, but his hands were clean. He was innocent. He was not guilty because he had nothing to do with robbing the bank. He was just a medic who had gone along to give first aid in case somebody got hurt. If necessary he might have saved a life.

"What do you think, Sami, the judge will say?" I asked. "Will he say he's he guilty or not? Don't you think the judge will declare him guilty because he knew what the men were going to do? He had agreed to be part of the team. To be sure, he didn't blow up the safe nor scoop up the money, but the lookout men were just watching the street. They didn't do any robbing, either. The driver didn't do any robbing."

Sami didn't say anything. He was thinking.

So I went on. "Surely the judge will find all ten men equally guilty, because they worked as a team to rob the bank. Everybody's job was different, but the purpose was the same—to rob the bank.

"Now, Sami, if a judge on earth will find our first-aid man guilty, how much more will the Judge in heaven find him guilty? If even a man (the judge) says he's guilty, how much more will God say he's guilty!"

I was finished. I rested my case. I thought that might be the end of the discussion. To my surprise, Sami spoke again. He said, "Now let me tell you a story, the same one you told only different."

He proceeded to tell the story of the ten men going to rob a bank just as I had told it. But then he said, "There was one man who had a first-aid kit and training as a medic. This man was already in the bank when the others came to rob it. In fact, he was upstairs and could hear the commotion down below when they blew up the safe."

"Hold it right there, Sami," I interrupted. "How did the first-aid man get into the bank before the others got there? What was he doing upstairs when the others were downstairs?"

"Let me finish the story," Sami said. "It'll all be clear in a moment. You see, the first-aid man is Swiss. The other nine aren't. Maybe they're Americans. They're now coming to rob the bank. You might say the bank is Switzerland. They're coming to attack the bank, to attack Switzerland. The first-aid man is already in the bank, in Switzerland, because he's Swiss.

"Now, when he hears the explosion of the cracked safe, he also hears groaning. Someone's hurt. So he asks himself what he should do. Fall on his knees and pray for the wounded men? Or grab his first-aid kit and run down to help?

"He went downstairs to give first aid to the wounded men," I replied. "Is that how you see yourself, Sami? You're a soldier in the Swiss army, but you're a medic."

Sami agreed. I did understand. First, others, like the bank robbers, would have to attack Switzerland. Switzerland would never attack another country but only defend itself. Second, men in the Army Medical Corps, like Sami, are trained in first aid. Their job is to save lives, never to take one.

"So you see," Sami concluded, "the real question for us isn't whether or not to be in the Swiss army. The real question is whether, according to your story, we should stay upstairs and just pray for the men wounded and dying downstairs. Or whether we should go down and try to save their lives."

I had to think a long time about that one. I still felt the first-aid fellow was part of a bad lot. He was a member of a team that wasn't solving problems the Jesus way. But for the moment I had nothing more to say. Sami and I agreed to talk some more another time. He hadn't really convinced me and I knew I hadn't convinced him. But we're friends, good friends. That's why we can talk about things like this.

"Let's meet again tomorrow," Sami said, "and talk about Henri Dunant and the Red Cross. Do you know why the Swiss flag and the logo of the Red Cross look almost alike? Only the colors are reversed."

I didn't know. I looked forward to having Sami explain that to me.

CHAPTER 5

Henri Dunant and the Red Cross

Sami Gerber and I met again the next day. He drank coffee and I drank tea. I like milk in my tea. It's the British way.

"Shall I tell you about Dunant?" he asked. "Jean Henri Dunant and the Red Cross.

"It may help you understand better what we were talking about yesterday. Remember? About being a medic in the Swiss army. And being a Christian."

I said I'd love to hear the story. Sami poured himself another cup and began. This is the story he told.

June 24, 1859, was a lovely day. Henri Dunant got up in the morning and pulled the window shades up to let in the bright sunshine. He looked out to his beloved Swiss Alps in the distance. Once more he realized how wonderful it was to be at home in beautiful Switzerland. He opened the window wide to the fresh air. The chirping of birds filled the room with happy melodies.

"Jean Henri Dunant," he said aloud to himself, "you're a lucky man. For 31 years this has been your home. What joy and peace—"

He didn't finish. He heard loud, excited voices in the street below. He dressed quickly and went outside. People were beginning to gather in the street. They were all talking at once. In the confusion, Henri heard the words "fighting" and "war." He heard the people talk about the Austrians and the French. Somebody mentioned the Italians. These were all people from countries around Henri's beloved little Switzerland.

He stayed just long enough to hear that the fighting was going on in Italy, just south of the Swiss border. He also heard that it was called the Battle of Solferino.

Then he dashed back into the house. Quickly he grabbed a few things for a trip and said good-bye to his family. He told them not to wait for him in the evening. He might be a long time. He was going to see the fighting.

When he got there he saw soldiers. Soon he recognized three different uniforms—French, Austrian, and Italian. The soldiers were fighting on the side of a hill. The hill was just outside the town of Castiglione. It seemed to Henri that everybody was shooting at everybody else. He saw men get hit by the bullets, throw up their arms, give a horrible cry, then fall to the ground. Sometimes they would lie still. He knew they were dead.

But many of the men didn't lie still. They rolled on the ground after they fell. They tried to get up again but couldn't. They pulled themselves along on their elbows, like a wounded animal with a broken back. They tried to crawl to a safe place. But there was no safe place.

More men fell to the ground. Soon they were falling on top of each other. Henri saw one man, who had been killed instantly, fall right on top of a badly wounded man. The wounded man was bleeding heavily. He was so weakened by loss of blood that he didn't have the strength to move the dead body off. He just lay there, groaning, with the wounds in his body and the dead man on top. He continued to bleed.

Henri had never seen anything like this. It turned his stomach; several times that day he vomited. But what upset him the most was that he couldn't get close to the wounded men to help them. All he could do was watch them fall to the ground when the bullets hit. He knew there must be many among them who weren't dead. He also knew that if nobody helped them, and stopped their bleeding, they would probably be dead by evening.

Henri didn't know then that he was seeing more than 40,000 casualties. They were spread over the fields as far as he could see.

Finally it got too dark for the soldiers to fight, so they left the battlefield. Henri also left and went into the nearby village of Castiglione. Here he asked people to go with him to the battlefield to help the wounded men.

He was talking to ordinary citizens, farmers and bakers and such, but they responded at once and followed Henri. They spent all night out there, giving as much first aid as they could. Henri and his helpers tried to save as many lives as possible.

After Henri got home he couldn't forget what he had seen and experienced. One day he sat down at his desk and wrote what he called *A Memory of Solferino*. In it he described seeing the horrible experience of that battle, especially the plight of the wounded men. He suggested that every country should have a relief society, a kind of emergency aid service to help wounded soldiers.

He didn't suggest that all countries should stop fighting and killing each other. He probably knew they wouldn't listen to him anyway. But they did listen to his suggestion about an emergency service to aid wounded soldiers. They all liked that idea.

They also liked his suggestion that they not take care of only their own wounded. Henri thought all wounded men, whether friends or enemies, should receive first aid. Then they should be taken as quickly as possible to the nearest hospital.

In 1864, only five years after the Battle of Solferino, the first such rescue society was organized in Geneva, Switzerland. Soon more countries joined the society. They called it the Red Cross. But everybody forgot about Henri Dunant, its founder. They even forgot why it was called the Red Cross.

"Sami, that's a fascinating story," I said. "But tell me, why was it called the Red Cross?"

"Because Jean Henri Dunant was a Swiss citizen.

Look at that Swiss flag outside." I saw it gently waving in the breeze.

"What do you see?" Sami asked.

"A white cross in a red field," I replied.

"Exactly," Sami continued. "Now when they thought about a logo for the new organization they just took the Swiss flag and reversed the colors. They made the cross red and the field white. That's why it's been called the Red Cross ever since."

But people forgot all about Henri Dunant. For years nobody talked about him nor the good thing he had done in starting the Red Cross.

Actually he did many more good things. He was one of the men who started the worldwide YMCA, the Young Men's Christian Association. He worked to abolish slavery. He helped the Jews get a homeland. And he encouraged the nations to disarm. To stop fighting.

Then one day in 1895 a newspaperman rediscovered him. Suddenly the name of Henri Dunant was on the front pages of all the newspapers. The Swiss were especially proud of him. In 1901 he was given the very first Nobel peace prize. It was 42 years after the Battle of Solferino and his suggestion to do something for the wounded soldiers.

Sami had finished his story. He had finished his coffee long ago. I thanked him for all he had told me. It had been most interesting and helpful.

And suddenly it was all clear to me—this business of being a soldier, a medic, and a Christian. The story had helped me sort it out. Now I knew why I could also be a medic, but not a medic in the army. Like Henri Dunant, I could be a medic outside the army.

I knew saving life was always right. But I also knew it wasn't right for two men to agree, for example, to go out together, the one with a gun and the other with a first-aid kit. It made no sense at all for the two men to work as a team, the one killing and wounding, the other giving first aid.

"Thank you so much, Sami," I said. "This has been very helpful. You are my friend indeed. Let's meet again and continue our discussion."

CHAPTER 6

Here Stood Kandanos*

*T*he bishop was a very gracious host. The meal had been excellent, the discussion stimulating. He reached for the basket of Greek oranges grown in his own orchard. He selected the nicest one for me.

I loved to watch him go through this ritual at the close of every meal. He'd pick up an orange, examine it carefully, then place it back in the basket. It wasn't good enough. He'd pick up another, look at it, look at me, then—just when I thought he was going to give it to me—shake his head and return it. He was looking for the perfect orange. It was his way of honoring his guest, his way of saying, "I am glad you came to Crete."

Bishop Irineos arose from the table and stood behind his chair. He made the sign of the cross, as Orthodox believers do, and said a prayer of thanks-

---

* Pronounced Kóndonos

giving. He always prayed before and after each meal. As we left the dining room to walk in his garden, I could hear the gentle lapping of Mediterranean waves. Through the trees I could see clear blue water. We walked side by side for some time, chatting.

Suddenly he stopped, turned to me, and asked, "Will you do it? Please don't say no."

I told him I would think about his invitation to send some of our young workers to Crete.

"Yes, yes," he interjected eagerly, "think about it. But also pray about it. We need help. Look at our poor island now. It was not always like this. Once when the apostle Paul landed here. . . ."

He didn't finish the sentence. "Now you are here." We both laughed when he said it that way.

"Then is not now, and I am not Paul," I said, teasing him.

"That's right, of course," he said in his gentle way. "But look what your young people could do for us in Crete. We have a good climate and lots of sunshine. But our people have no work. And why is there no work? Why are more and more young people leaving this lovely island? Paul could make tents, you know. But our young people have no skills, they have not been trained.

"Soon Crete will be an island of old people. If you could just send us a few craftsmen to train our young people. With new skills they would find new jobs. Then they would stay here. Perhaps you could start a vocational training school."

The bishop had spoken like a man who loves his

people. And he certainly loved his island. I asked him to tell me more about it.

"The island of Crete is a part of mainland Greece," he began. "But we are a rather independent lot. I guess that comes with living on an island. The Cretans are a friendly people, but they do have a history of violence. We still have blood feuds and vendettas."

"You know," he explained, "the kind of grudges that can fester between two families. They actually continue from one generation to another."

I told him I had heard of a fourteen-year-old student killing his teacher in the classroom in order to "restore the honor" of his family. Many years before someone in the teacher's family had killed someone in this student's family.

"That's exactly the way it works," responded the bishop sadly. "And now it's that teacher's family's turn to get even again with the student's family. Sometimes these vendettas continue over many, many years."

I found that interesting but also sad and disturbing. I didn't know how I should ask my next question, but I did want to understand the Cretans better. "Is that perhaps why Paul wrote to Titus, whom he had left in Crete to take care of the church, that a church leader should be 'blameless . . . not . . . quick-tempered or violent'?"

Bishop Irineos smiled. "Many people who know nothing about Crete know about that because it's in the Bible. But that was almost 2,000 years ago.

"But, of course, Paul was right. Not only should

church leaders but any followers of Jesus reject quick tempers or violence. And now I suppose you're going to tell me the rest of what Paul wrote about us Cretans? How he quoted one of our poets who had said: 'Cretans are always liars, wicked beasts, and lazy gluttons.' "

"No, no!" I protested. "I wasn't going to say that. It certainly isn't true now and I don't suppose it was all true then."

Now it was the bishop's turn to tease. He asked wistfully, "How do you know it's not true today?"

"Because I know one Cretan who is not like that! You! And I'm sure there are many more like you," I shot back.

Half seriously and half in jest he told me not to be too sure. "Cretans may not be liars and certainly aren't beasts but they have always been fighters," he said. "There's a violent streak in them. Cretans are proud of being fighters.

"But come now, I want to show you our beautiful island," he continued, opening the door to the car.

We drove around for several hours. The entire island is only 160 miles long and 40 miles wide. Much of it is mountainous. Now he didn't need to tell me any longer that the island was beautiful. I could see it with my own eyes.

I also saw how the people loved their bishop. In every village they crowded around the car. They kissed his hand and gave him little gifts. Sometimes it was five eggs, another time some fruit. He accepted it gratefully and blessed them.

Suddenly we came to a large open place that was

neither field nor meadow. It looked rather strange. Building material, like broken bricks and stones, were strewn over the landscape. As far as I could see, there was no grass, no crops, no buildings. Only rubble. Even the sheep, which seemed to be everywhere, were absent. We stood silently for a long time, gazing at this desolate area. Finally I asked: "What happened here? An earthquake?"

"No earthquake," replied the bishop sadly. "Much worse. Come, read what it says on this plaque." He led me to a monument, a large boulder, on which a metal plaque had been fastened. The following was engraved on it in Greek and in German:

> "Here stood Kandanos. It was demolished because Cretans killed a German soldier."

"Tell me about it," I asked Bishop Irineos. "What happened?"

We walked back to the car. He was silent. I could see it hurt him to talk about it. At last he began.

"It was during World War II. Germany and Italy attacked Crete from the air. They dropped bombs. But no soldiers landed on the island. Helping us to defend the island were British soldiers as well as soldiers from faraway Australia and New Zealand.

"At the end of April 1941, mainland Greece fell. The Germans had won the war against our people there. They set up their own government in Athens. The Greek king and his government fled. But the Germans still did not have this island. Crete was still free.

"Then came May 20, 1941. The sun wasn't yet up, but the eastern sky was already tinted orange and yellow. In this early dawn we saw the Germans coming. They came in airplanes. But not like before, when they had come in two or three planes and dropped bombs on us. Now they came with too many planes to count. The air was filled with planes. The people wondered what all that noise up in the air was about. They ran outside and stood on their yards and in the streets, looking up.

"Most of us thought they were just flying over Crete to go somewhere else. Of course they couldn't land in Crete because we had only three little airports with short runways. And the Germans had already destroyed those with their bombs. There were hundreds and hundreds of airplanes up there. Then it happened—"

Bishop Irineos stopped and looked away. I saw him take his handkerchief and wipe his eyes. I didn't know whether he would continue. The memory of that day was obviously very painful. I waited. Once he started again but didn't continue because his voice broke. To give him time I walked back to the plaque and read again, "Here stood Kandanos."

The bishop cleared his throat. He apologized for stopping in the middle of the story and continued. "You cannot imagine what happened that morning when all the Cretans had run out of their houses and stood in their yards and in the streets looking up into the sky. We had never in all our life seen so many airplanes. We were still wondering whether they would keep on going or drop bombs on us—when it happened.

"It was all so sudden. One moment we looked up and saw the sky filled with planes. The next moment we saw the sky filled with parachutes. Thousands and thousands of men, German soldiers, were coming down with those parachutes. Many more were coming down on gliders. They were invading our island. They would occupy Crete—just as they had already occupied the mainland of Greece.

"There was nobody to organize a quick resistance and nobody to give orders. But that wasn't necessary. All the people knew what to do. They all had the same idea—kill as many Germans as possible. Kill them as soon as they land on the ground. No, better still, kill them even before they land.

"Not only the men but also the women immediately ran back into their houses to get some weapons with which to kill the Germans. Some had guns, but many had only knives and axes. Some ran into the barns to get their pitchforks and machetes. Some simply picked up steel pipes and iron rods to use as spears and clubs.

"As the Germans came floating down, and before they hit the ground, the Cretans were already upon them. Men, women, and even teenage children tried to kill as many Germans as possible. It was a terrible slaughter. Dead bodies were all over the place. There was blood everywhere. But the Germans kept coming. There were so many of them. There seemed to be no end. The Cretans couldn't possibly win."

Again the bishop stopped. I almost wished I hadn't asked about this. But if I was going to understand these people, I needed to know.

At last he continued: "In all, about 7,000 German soldiers landed in Crete that day. However, the fighting continued into the night and all next day. Many Cretans were able to sneak away and hide in the mountains and among the rocks. At night they came out and ambushed the Germans. All the men, and even boys, became freedom fighters or guerrillas. They fought fiercely for eleven days.

"On the night of May 31, 1941, all the British, Australian, and New Zealand soldiers left Crete. They jumped into boats and quietly slipped away, leaving us Greeks alone. We had to surrender. Crete collapsed, just as mainland Greece had collapsed. The losses on both sides were enormous. The Germans lost more than 12,000 men."

Again Bishop Irineos stopped. It was a bloodcurdling story. Then I remembered that he had said only a little while before: Cretans weren't liars, wicked beasts, and gluttons. But they were fighters. The bishop's story certainly confirmed this. It also helped me understand why the Cretans hated the Germans. I had heard them say more than once that the only good German was a dead German. Now I knew why.

But the good bishop still hadn't told me about Kandanos. Why was Kandanos destroyed and why was that plaque put up saying, "Here stood Kandanos"? The more I thought about it, the surer I was that it hadn't been destroyed on that horrible day when the Germans landed on Crete. On that day it was all hand-to-hand combat. Whatever had destroyed those houses in Kandanos had to be bigger than a hand grenade or a machine gun. But what? And why?

I decided to wait. In his own time the bishop would tell me. Not to push him on that would be my way of showing respect. He asked me to get back in the car. He wanted to take me to a monastery at Kolumbari.

The monastery was like most others I had seen in different countries, a cluster of ancient buildings surrounded by a high wall. Monks—the men who had promised to live only for God, to remain poor, not to marry, and to help other people—walked about in brown tunics. Everybody had a job to do.

The bishop spoke quietly to one of the monks, who immediately disappeared. Minutes later he came back with tea and small cakes for us. The abbot, the man in charge of the monastery, came and sat with us. We sat at a small table in the open courtyard completely surrounded by massive stone buildings. I thought perhaps the buildings could be used for a vocational training school.

"Do you use all these buildings?" I asked the abbot.

"Yes we do," he replied, then added, "in one way or another."

I wondered what that was supposed to mean: "In one way or another."

I felt like walking and exploring. I asked the abbot whether he would show me the inside of

some of the larger buildings. What seemed an innocent question to me was apparently not quite so
harmless to him. He hesitated before speaking.

Then he turned to the bishop and asked, "Is it
okay?"

The bishop replied: "I have already told our
guest a lot. You might as well tell him the whole
story."

The abbot got up and said, "Come, we will show
you the buildings."

We walked to the first building. It was massive.
Built of stone, it must have weathered many a Mediterranean storm through the centuries. The windows were small and closed by outside shutters. It
was neither house nor barn, and as we walked to-
ward it I wondered if it was a workshop. It seemed
to me a hundred monks could have worked in there
with wood or iron, leather or cloth, or some other
material.

The abbot reached for the keys hanging in a ring
from his "belt," a cord around his waist. He seemed
to fumble a bit as he tried different keys, explaining
as he did so that they didn't go into this building
often. At last he got the right key. The old iron lock
turned with difficulty and a squeak. He pulled the
huge door open and stood back.

To my surprise we couldn't go into the building.
From floor to roof, and from wall to wall, the entire
building was filled with boxes. Narrow and longish
boxes made of wood. They were unpainted. For a
moment an absolutely impossible thought flashed
through my mind. But I didn't say anything. To me

these boxes looked like coffins. That was ridiculous and impossible, of course. What would anybody do with hundreds and perhaps thousands of coffins? The bishop saw my surprise.

"What are these boxes?" I asked.

"Coffins!" replied the bishop. "Coffins with German soldiers. Dead Germans, all of them."

It took me a while to get used to the idea of standing in front of this strange cemetery. It was even more startling than the pyramid of German skulls we had seen a few hours earlier, near the sign that said, "Here stood Kandanos."

The abbot explained that his monastery was storing the coffins until the German government made up its mind what to do with them.

"But this is fifteen years after the war!" I finally exclaimed. "Doesn't it disturb you to have all these . . . these . . . *Germans* here with you?"

He smiled and said, "They're dead. We're not afraid of dead Germans." He closed the door, fumbled with the keys, and turned the squeaky lock. Then he asked, "Want to see more buildings?"

I didn't. This was enough for one afternoon.

Turning to the bishop, the abbot asked: "Will you join us tomorrow for our *Oxi* (pronounced 'oyhee') service?" Bishop Irineos said he would let the abbot know. The abbot kissed the bishops's hand. We said good-bye and drove off.

In the car I asked: "Tell me, bishop, what did the abbot mean by *Oxi* service? I know, of course, that *oxi* in Greek means *no*, but what is a *No Service*? Why would the monks be celebrating a *No Service* tomorrow?"

The bishop smiled his usual kindly smile and replied: "This also has to do with the Germans. Remember how they took the mainland of Greece and dropped bombs on us in World War II? Remember how they invaded Crete by parachutes and gliders on the morning of May 20, 1941?

"Now a few days before they did that the German military asked us to surrender. They said if we would give ourselves up peacefully and let them occupy Crete, there would be no bombing and no bloodshed. Nobody would get killed. You also remember I told you the Cretans are fighters. Well, they didn't need a long time to make up their minds what to reply to the Germans.

"Quick as that they shot back the answer: 'Oxi! No!' So the Germans took the island by force. But ever since then we celebrate Oxi Day. And tomorrow is Oxi Day, the day on which we said 'No!' to the Germans. We'll ring our church bells. We'll stop working. We'll celebrate. That's the kind of people we are."

We had just passed through another village and were about to pass the Kandanos area again when the bishop said: "I don't think I have told you yet what happened here. Come, let's walk back again to that monument."

By now I had not only photographed it, I had etched the words on my mind: "Here stood Kandanos. It was demolished because Cretans killed a German soldier."

"Kandanos was a typical village," the bishop began. "It was the kind of village we just passed through. There were from 300 to 400 people living here. Most were farmers. Some were fishermen, tradesmen, merchants, teachers, and a lot of retired people. All had their sheep and goats, their oranges and olive trees. And all belonged, of course, to the church. Everybody in Crete belongs to the Orthodox Church.

"They were peasant people who loved their families and loved Crete. When the German soldiers came and occupied our island, many of our men and older boys continued to resist them. The Germans said they were guerrillas. We said they were freedom fighters.

"One night a German officer was on the road with his jeep. It was near Kandanos, not far from this spot. Some of our freedom fighters ambushed the jeep, shot the officer dead, and set the jeep on fire. Then they disappeared.

"The next morning many German soldiers and officers came to Kandanos. They demanded to know who had done that. Of course nobody would tell. So they rounded up every man and boy 13 years and older. They lined them up, and shot them dead. All of them!

"When they had done that they came with bulldozers and destroyed every house and building in the village. In the morning of that day, the people had gone to work. Children had gone to school. The storekeeper had opened his little shop as usual. Women had cooked and washed. In the evening, the village was rubble. Just the way you see it here.

"Some days later, the Germans came with this

plaque and put it up. It was supposed to be a warning to others. That's why it says: 'Here stood Kandanos. It was demolished because Cretans killed a German soldier.' "

"How awful! How shocking!" I said. "And how unfair. Your people killed one German officer. The Germans killed hundreds of your men and boys."

The bishop was silent. Then he asked, "Have you ever heard of a war that was fair? Is not every war unfair?"

As we turned away from the monument, the bishop abruptly changed the subject. "Are you going to send us somebody to teach our young people vocational skills?" he asked.

"Perhaps you have an electrician, or somebody who understands engines and cars. We could also use somebody who works with iron, a metallurgist. He could teach our young people how to weld and make iron grills. Railings and all kinds of things."

I told him I would give it serious thought. I would pray about it and share it with my friends at Mennonite Central Committee. Then I would let him know.

By evening we were back again in Kolumbari. It had been a full day. I had learned a lot. Now we had finished supper, except dessert. Once more I was intrigued with the way the bishop selected the best orange for me. When the fourth one seemed just right, he handed it to me.

I reached out to take it. But he held it, looked at me a moment, and said, "There is more. I must tell you more. It's true we Cretans are fighters and hate the Germans. But we also love the church."

I didn't quite catch the connection between the orange he was holding in his hand, hating the Germans, being fighters, and loving the church. What was clear was that he expected a response from me.

Since I couldn't very well take the orange out of his hand, and since I didn't want to talk anymore about the Germans, I said: "That's wonderful! My people love the church too."

"But you're different," he continued. "You're not Orthodox. If you send us your people, I suppose they'll be against Mary, the saints, and tradition."

He had said all of that so fast I hardly had time to process it. What I did catch, however, was that he thought we would be *against* something. Something important to them.

"Against what?" I asked. "Would you say that again, please?"

"Against Mary," he said. "You Mennonites don't make much of Mary, the mother of Jesus, do you? You don't have pictures and icons of her. You don't pray to her. But my people do. I teach them to. For us Mary is very important. It has just occurred to me that if you send us your teachers they might say things against Mary that would offend my people.

"The same thing is true about the saints. You don't even have saints to pray to like we have, do you? If you send us teachers that speak lightly about our saints, my Orthodox people wouldn't take kindly to that. You see, we even have saints' days. Celebrating the birthday of a saint, like St. Paul or St. Peter, is more important to our people than celebrating their own birthday."

I could see the good bishop was thinking. The more he thought, the more concerned he got. It seemed, in fact, he was more than just concerned; he was deeply worried. On the one hand, he wanted us to come to Crete; on the other hand, he couldn't see how we could work happily together if we believed so differently.

"And there is tradition," he added. "You know how important tradition is for us in the Orthodox church! When something has been done a certain way for hundreds of years, we call that tradition. It becomes important for us to continue doing it exactly the same way.

"In fact, for us the Bible and tradition are almost equally important. If we want to know what's right or wrong we don't only ask what the Bible says, we also ask what our tradition says. But you people don't think tradition is that important, do you?"

Now what was I to say? He was right. Neither I nor my people prayed to Mary or the saints. And we certainly didn't think that just because something had been done a certain way for hundreds of years, it was therefore right and couldn't be changed. We did have our traditions, but they were less important. Certainly not equal to the Bible. Silently I prayed for the Lord to give me the right answer.

"Bishop Irineos," I finally began, "you are right. We don't worship Mary or the saints. We don't believe tradition is as important as the Bible. But why talk about something we are *against*? Why not talk about something we are *for?* Something we both agree on. Something you and we have in common."

"Yes, yes, I like that," he said eagerly. "But what would that be? What do you have in mind? What do we have in common?"

"Why, Bishop Irineos, I think I speak for our people when I say that, first of all, we also love the church. Just as your Orthodox people love it. Even more important, we love Jesus, as do your people."

The bishop beamed. He seemed very happy. As he relaxed, he suddenly realized he was still hanging on to the orange. He had completely forgotten it. He handed it to me. Thanking him, I continued.

"Bishop Irineos, let me make a proposal. If we send our teachers and helpers to Crete, they'll come with clear instructions not to speak against Mary, the saints, or tradition. They'll speak about Jesus Christ. He's the one we love and serve. He's also the one your people love and serve. So we have nothing to disagree about or get upset about.

"Let's see how long we can keep that up. Perhaps one or two years. When we've finished talking about Jesus and think the time has come to be against the things that are important to you, we can decide what to do next. How do you like that?"

"A splendid idea," said the bishop. "I like it very much. Let Jesus bring us together. And I'm sure he'll also keep us together."

The next day I flew back to my office in Frankfurt, Germany. My committee agreed that sending young people to Crete, the way Bishop Irineos had requested, would be just fine. The money for the program was available. All we needed was to find the right volunteers.

So we looked around. We asked in the churches and in the colleges, but nobody volunteered. Then we put it into our church papers. We waited, but nobody came forward. It seemed that just then there was nobody available with the right kind of training who was also free to go to Crete.

After many months we found a young man in Ohio who was an electrician. He was Richard Kaufmann. Richard said he would love to go to Crete to teach everything he knew about electricity. He would be glad to teach the young people there how to wire a house. He would show them how to repair all kinds of electrical appliances. But he would not be able to leave his job in Ohio for another six months.

That was good news and bad news. We wanted him to go at once. More and more young people were leaving Crete because they had no jobs. And the reason they had no jobs was that they had no skills. There was nobody there to train them.

Then Klaus applied. Klaus Froese said he had learned how to work with iron. He was a metallurgist. He said he could teach young people welding—which the people would need to repair farm machinery, oxcarts, and wagons. He could also teach grille work—a skill useful when building railings for steps in houses. In fact, he could do just about anything with iron. Klaus was also ready to go almost at once.

This was good news! Furthermore, Klaus

wouldn't have to travel all the way from North America, he was already in Europe. Klaus lived in North Germany, near Hamburg. At that time more and more European young people were joining the Mennonite Central Committee (MCC) as volunteers. We were very happy for that. And Klaus seemed an answer to our prayers.

As I looked through his file I began to realize that here was an almost perfect volunteer. He was 21 years old. He had a needed skill. He was healthy and strong. He looked, in fact, like an Olympic athlete. He had already worked on his own so he had experience and could teach others. He was a church member in good standing.

All the people we asked about Klaus said that he was a wonderful young man. They said MCC and Crete would be very fortunate to have him. He loved people and the Lord. He was willing to go to Crete for two years and ready to leave as soon as we called for him. What more could we ask for?

However, before saying yes to Klaus, I wanted to meet him myself. I wanted to see whether all the wonderful things I had heard about him were true.

So he came to Frankfurt. He stayed with us for several days. Everybody liked him. He certainly seemed to be the answer to the problem in Crete. Except for one thing. Would he go alone or would he want to wait for the electrician, Richard Kaufmann, from Ohio?

"Why wait?" he said. "I'm ready to go now. I won't be lonely." I liked that spirit. Klaus had spunk. We sent him to Crete. Alone.

About a month later, I was in my office, quietly reading letters and reports. Suddenly something hit me. It almost knocked me off my chair. It was as if someone had punched me hard in the stomach. I slouched forward, put my head in my arms on the desk, and groaned.

"Peter Dyck, what have you done!" I moaned again and again to myself. "How could you do that? How could you be so stupid? How could you send Klaus Froese to Crete? Klaus is a GERMAN! Peter Dyck, how could you forget that the Cretans *hate* the Germans!" Hadn't they told me themselves the only good German was a dead German? I was sick. Poor Klaus.

I was still moaning and groaning when my secretary walked in. "What's the matter, Peter?" she asked. "Are you sick?"

"It's worse than that," I replied. "I've done a terrible thing."

"Whatever it is, it surely can't be that bad," she said, trying to comfort me. She didn't know.

"It *is* that bad! I sent Klaus Froese into the lions' den. They'll eat him alive. Poor Klaus. Why didn't I think about his being a German. And such a fine young man he was."

"Don't say 'was.' " My secretary shuddered. "Klaus *is* a fine young man. Perhaps the lions haven't eaten him. At least not yet."

The story of Daniel and King Darius flashed through my mind. I remembered reading that after Darius threw Daniel into the lions' den he couldn't sleep all night. It bothered him terribly. Early the next morning he ran to the den and called down: "Daniel, O Daniel! Are you alright?"

I had to do the same. I had to find out at once and for myself how Klaus was. Quickly I made plans. I was going to visit the other volunteers in the north of Greece, in Macedonia, in two weeks anyway. Why not move the schedule up and go now? Go to Macedonia and see the team there, then take that quick hop to Crete to see Klaus.

Three days later the bishop met me at the small airport in Chania. I wasted no time, I came straight to the point. "How is Klaus?" I asked, and hoped my voice didn't sound too anxious.

"Klaus is fine. He's learning Greek and has started his vocational training school."

I was relieved, of course. But I wanted to hear directly from Klaus that he was okay. The time came after the evening meal with the bishop. We were alone at last in Klaus's small room.

"Now tell me, Klaus, how are you? How do the people treat you? What are your problems? Tell me everything." All my questions just tumbled out.

I sat back to listen. I wondered if Klaus had seen that pyramid of German skulls yet. Did he know about the thousands of German bodies in the coffins at the monastery? Had somebody already taken him to the site of the former Kandanos? Had he read the plaque: "Here stood Kandanos"? But I said nothing. I just waited. Then Klaus began.

"The people are wonderful. I like my students. I have a good relationship with Bishop Irineos. I am happy in my work. But you asked me to tell you about my problems. Okay, I will."

Now it's coming, I thought. Now he's going to tell me the people are wonderful but allergic to Germans. He's going to tell me that, yes, he likes his students. But they hate him because he's German. Then he's going to ask why I hadn't thought about all that before sending him to Crete. And could he please go back to Germany with me.

I was still thinking these thoughts, waiting for Klaus to tell me his problems, when he reached for the hymnbook.

"Here's my problem," he said, holding up the book. I didn't understand. Was that supposed to be funny? How could a hymnbook be a problem? And we weren't talking about that sort of thing. Surely the Cretans were his problem. Being a German was his problem.

"I can't sing," Klaus said, almost as though he had been accused of something. "I hate singing solos. And they sound awful!"

"Klaus Froese! What in the world are you talking about? Who is asking you to sing solos? When? Where? I don't understand a word of what you are saying," I replied in surprise.

"You, Peter, and the MCC are asking me to sing solos," he almost sobbed. "And I tell you, Peter, I can't sing. It sounds terrible and I don't even like to hear myself."

Now I knew Klaus was serious, this was no joke. But what did he mean? How could he say I and the MCC were asking him to sing solos? He was still talking in riddles.

"If you could just tell me that I don't have to sing solos anymore," he asked, "that would solve my problem. It would make me very happy. Couldn't you make an exception? Just this once?"

At last we got to the bottom of his problem. It all became clear to me when he produced the MCC Handbook. There it was, in clear print: "Standards for MCC Workers." These standards, or instructions, had come indirectly from me and several other MCC workers many years ago. Now it all came back.

It was during World War II, about 1943, when MCC was sending out more and more volunteers. The committee felt it needed what it called "standards" for all workers, a list of do's and don'ts.

Four of us were rookies in England at the time. We thought it was a good idea. In fact, we thought we ought to make a suggestion about these "standards" ourselves. So we wrote our central office, suggesting that all MCC workers should have daily devotions. We also suggested that these devotions should consist of reading the Bible, saying prayers, and singing hymns. The committee liked that and printed it in the MCC Handbook.

Now Klaus Froese didn't take that MCC Handbook and its standards for volunteers lightly. He wanted to be a good MCC worker. He wanted to obey all the rules. So he had daily devotions, he read his Bible, and he prayed. That was no problem. He would have done that anyway.

But when Handbook told him to sing, *that* was a problem. He was, in his own words, "a lousy sing-er." He could hardly stand listening to his own voice. He was sure the angels in heaven used earplugs when he started to sing. The fact that all his singing had to be solos, since he was alone, just made it that much worse.

When Klaus finally made all that clear to me, I laughed so hard my sides began to hurt. And to think this was Klaus's biggest problem! I realized once more that Klaus was really something else! No wonder his students liked him.

In some ways Klaus was very German. He was, for example, thorough. He was a careful worker. He hated slipshod work. He was conscientious. Klaus also followed orders, obeying almost to a fault. Like singing those solos. Oh, how we did laugh! Over and over he thanked me. "No more solos!" he exulted. "No more listening to a croaking frog trying to sing!"

At the end of the first year, Richard Kaufmann from Ohio joined Klaus. Richard taught electricity. Klaus and Richard, the German and the American, were a good team. We also sent Orpha Zimmerli to teach the girls and women home economics. She went equipped with a knitting machine and other basic tools.

The bishop was pleased with this *troika*, this trio. He confidentially told me more than once how wonderful the three were. Except for one thing— the fellows didn't take enough students. Bishop Irineos thought they should have at least twenty each, forty in all. So many young people were waiting to be trained.

But Klaus thought six or seven each was enough. Klaus was used to the apprentice system, a way of teaching another person through practical experience. In the apprentice system, teacher and student work together. The teacher doesn't simply lecture in a classroom. They did, actually, start out with 16 boys and young men. The only training any of them had had was six years of elementary school.

Once, for a long time, I watched Klaus teach. I liked the way he passed on to the young people the skills he himself had learned. He did it in three stages. First he told them what they were going to make and how they were to make it. Then he showed them what he meant by actually making it himself. All the fellows watched him. Finally, he told them to try making it themselves.

In one of his first lessons, their job was simply to sharpen a piece of iron. He asked them to shape the end of a blunt rod into a point. They would have to hold the iron rod in one hand and the hammer in the other. First the iron was heated red hot. Then it was placed on the anvil.

Now came the tricky part—to hit the tip of the glowing rod once, then give it a half turn, hit it again, turn it and hit again. Some caught on quickly and did it as Klaus did, with a rhythm. Hit and turn, hit and turn, until the blunt end became a sharp point. But others had more difficulty.

I saw Klaus go from one fellow to the other. Instead of telling them again how to do it, he simply put his own hands on top of the hands of the apprentice. Then they did it together. Klaus would guide the fellow's hands as he sang out: "Strike and turn, strike and turn, strike and turn." Gradually he would withdraw his own hands and the apprentice would continue on his own.

I was convinced that the apprentice system was a good way to teach vocational skills. The young people learned fast and enjoyed it. They also enjoyed their one-to-one relationship with Klaus. What's more, as soon as they graduated they got jobs. Not one young man from the so-called Klaus and Richard Vocational Training School remained unemployed. All over the island, and even on Greek mainland, people asked for young men whom Klaus and Richard had trained.

Already during their second year of instruction a wonderful thing happened. The government officially recognized the fledgling vocational training school. It came about in an interesting and unexpected way.

One day some of the young men came to Klaus with a question. They wondered if Klaus was going to give them a certificate when they graduated. They would like that. Klaus thought this was funny. He didn't tell them what he thought, but it seemed ridiculous. A certificate? An official document that would be recognized all over Greece? Of course it would be wonderful for the "graduates," but who was Klaus to give them such certificate?

But Klaus and Richard thought about it and discussed the idea with Bishop Irineos. If they were to give a certificate, the government would have to officially recognize their "school." To Klaus and Richard that seemed like reaching for the stars. And while a certificate would be a good thing, all they really wanted was to give the young men the best training they knew how.

But the bishop liked the idea of a diploma. So he talked to some people in the government about it. They sent out men to inspect this new "school." The officials looked into the program and talked with the young men. They also talked with Klaus and Richard.

They liked what they saw. Klaus and Richard were doing fine work. The government men talked a long time with the bishop. They had a plan.

How would the bishop like it, they asked, if the government not only gave the school official recognition, but also gave him a new and better building? How would he like it if the government gave him some more tools and equipment? Gave him money to run the school? And asked him to continue to head this Vocational Training School at Kastelli?

This was too good to be true! It was music to Bishop Irineos' ears. He had wanted to help his people get training, get jobs, and stay on the island. He hadn't expected his dream to become reality this fast. His prayers had been answered.

The people of Kastelli were also delighted. The students were happy. Their parents were grateful. And Klaus and Richard were overwhelmed.

Soon the new building was erected. More equipment, tools, and supplies were delivered. New teachers arrived. Some were young men Klaus and

Richard had trained themselves. And now, instead of 16 young men learning new skills and trades, there were 200.

But now the time had come for Klaus to return home. He had come to Crete in 1961. His time as a volunteer with MCC was up. But Klaus didn't walk into my office to say good-bye after two years of service in Crete. Instead, my secretary walked in with a letter from Bishop Irineos.

"Please don't take Klaus home," he wrote. "We need Klaus here more than he is needed anywhere else. Please let him stay."

There was another letter from Klaus in the same mail. In it, he told of the bishop and many other people begging him to stay. If it was alright with MCC, he would like to stay a second term.

Of course we let him stay. By now Klaus had learned two new languages, Greek and English. With the people of Crete he spoke Greek, but with Richard and Orpha he spoke English. All this in addition to a very full teaching schedule.

And he enjoyed an increasing round of social activities. People liked him and often invited him out. In one of his reports he wrote: "I have so many friends here. First there is the bishop and his priests. Then there are my fellow teachers. Then there are the students themselves and their families, not to mention the people of the town."

No wonder time flew for Klaus. Before he knew it, it was again the end of his term. Again the time had come to think about going back to Germany and home.

The years in Crete had been wonderful years for Klaus. He knew he had changed. He would never be the same. These had been years of learning as well as teaching. Years of growing and giving, accepting and reaching out. Klaus was happy and the bishop was thankful.

I talked with Bishop Irineos. "Remember the time I was afraid your young people might be against Mary, against the saints, and against tradition?" he asked. "Remember how you suggested we start by emphasizing Jesus? Your workers have been wonderful! Do you remember we agreed that when we were finished with Jesus we would decide what to do next?" He laughed a hearty laugh.

Then he turned serious. He took both my hands in his and said, "We're not nearly done with Jesus Christ, are we? Thank you. It's been wonderful!"

And if Klaus thought he was going to quietly pack his bags and leave Crete he was mistaken. He knew that there was something unusual going on. He caught people whispering when they thought he wasn't looking. A group seemed to be practicing something. Workers were building a platform in the town square. Whatever it was, it was their business. Klaus intended to teach till the last day.

But he didn't. The last week of his stay in Crete he didn't teach at all. He hardly got anything done. He was too busy going from one home to another for dinners. Too busy accepting invitations to all kinds of parties. Too busy celebrating.

Many of the people who invited him were his old friends, but there were also some he hardly knew.

Town and government officials wanted to shake his hand. Klaus didn't know what to make of it all. Everybody wanted him to know they appreciated him. Some said they loved him. Many had little gifts for him.

Finally Klaus's last day in Crete arrived. To his astonishment, the entire community of Kastelli ground to a halt. People filled the town square. There was singing. The band played. People on that platform began to deliver all kinds of speeches, thanking Klaus and praising him. Bishop Irineos spoke for the Orthodox church and said: "Klaus Froese came to us as a gift from God."

The mayor of Kastelli spoke and said, "When Klaus came, none of us knew him. We paid very little attention to him. Today he leaves us as a dear friend. We will all miss him." Many other people spoke. A man from the government made a speech.

Then came the big surprise. The mayor stepped up to the podium once more. It got very quiet. Apparently everybody knew what was going to happen. Except Klaus. He had no idea.

"Our dear friend Klaus Froese," the mayor began. "We debated in the town council what gift the town of Kastelli could give to you. There were many suggestions. We have chosen the one that seems to express the wish of all the people. We have decided we want to make you an honorary citizen of our town, Kastelli—" He paused, then said, "For the rest of your life!"

He got no further. The people cheered and cheered. The band struck up music. Several times

Klaus tried to respond. But every time he stepped to the microphone, the cheering broke out again. His students, standing off to one side in a group, beamed with pride. The mother of one of them, a poor widow, wept unashamedly for joy. People danced in the streets.

Klaus Froese had done what more than 15,000 armed soldiers could not do. He had captured the hearts of the people of Crete. They had accepted him as one of their own. They had made him an honorary citizen. For life. The love and humble service of one young man had melted all their hatred and defenses. And he was a German.

The monument with that shocking inscription, "Here stood Kandanos," is still there. Someone suggested erecting a monument at the vocational training school, with the inscription, "Here stood Klaus." It would have been fitting. But it wasn't necessary. Klaus stood in the hearts of the people of Crete.

When Klaus returned to Germany he didn't return to work with iron. He wanted to work with people. Instead of becoming a metallurgist, he became a social worker. Now he takes care of the more than 280,000 Greek migrant workers in Germany. He has been doing that for almost 25 years. He married Gudrun Wiebe, another German MCC worker in Greece, and they have two daughters.

From time to time they go on vacation. Where do they go? To Crete, of course, where Klaus still stands in the hearts of the people of Kastelli.

The Author

Peter J. Dyck, born in Russia, was a boy when the communist revolution swept the country. In 1927, when Peter was twelve, his parents emigrated with him and his eight siblings to Saskatchewan, Canada.

Dyck attended Rosthern Junior College (then called German-English Academy) and the University of Saskatchewan. He interrupted his formal studies to pastor several struggling churches in Sudbury, Ontario. Then in 1941 he went to England with Mennonite Central Committee (MCC) to serve World War II victims.

After the war, Dyck attended Goshen College (B.A.), Bethel College, Mennonite Biblical Seminary, and Bethel Theological Seminary (M.Div.). The University of Waterloo granted him an honorary doctoral degree.

Dyck has worked with MCC most of his life, in many countries and capacities. He has always had a

strong interest in the Soviet Union and has returned many times, ministering to believers and
trying to build bridges of goodwill between East
and West.

While in England, Dyck married Elfrieda Klassen,
another volunteer and Russian-born Mennonite who
had emigrated to Canada. She offered her nursing
skills to children hurt during the war. The Dycks
have two daughters, Ruth (Scott) and Rebecca.
They have five grandchildren.

To better serve thousands of refugees after World
War II, Peter was ordained to the ministry in 1947.
He was pastor of Eden Mennonite Church, Mound-
ridge, Kansas (1950-1957). He was interim pastor of
Kingview Mennonite Church, Scottdale, Pennsylva-
nia (1983-1985). For over a decade he served on
the Commission of Overseas Mission, the mission
board of the General Conference Mennonite
Church. He holds dual membership in the General
Conference Mennonite Church and the Mennonite
Church. Now retired in Akron, Pennsylvania, Dyck
spends his time speaking, writing, and storytelling.